Mary, Archetype of the Church

Mary, Archetype of the Church

Otto Semmelroth, S.J.

Translated by Maria von Eroes
and John Devlin

Introduction by Jaroslav Pelikan

SHEED AND WARD · NEW YORK

Originally published in German under the title
Urbild der Kirche by Echter-Verlag, Würzburg.

Contents

v

THE STRUCTURE OF THE MARIAN MYSTERY 113

Introduction

THEOLOGICAL LITERATURE in English, which is so meager in satisfactory books on Holy Baptism or on the Blessed Trinity, seems to be abundantly supplied with articles, monographs, and treatises on the Blessed Virgin Mary. George D. Smith's exposition of *Mary's Part in Our Redemption* was adjudged important enough to be translated into German; Juniper Carol's multi-volume *Mariology* is a veritable encyclopedia of Marian speculation and devotion; even the author of this "Introduction" has written about the historical and the ecumenical aspects of this doctrine.[1] Why, then, should another treatise on the Blessed Virgin by a German Jesuit be translated into English?

The basic answer would seem to be that Father Semmelroth's book is not just another treatise on the Blessed Virgin, but a study whose learning and originality qualify it for the attention of anyone interested in Christian doctrine, regardless of his ecclesiastical affiliation. Even more than Père Congar's provocative treatise on *Christ, Our Lady, and the Church*,[2] the present volume shows how embedded Mariology is not only in Roman Catholic theology and piety, but in the entire tradition of orthodox Christianity. This it does by outlining the implications of Mariology for the doctrine of the Church and for the doctrine of the person and work of Jesus Christ. Therefore those who believe that the dogmatic promulgations of 1854 and 1950 are the major obstacle to Christian understanding between Protestantism and Roman Catholicism, as well as those who smile superciliously at all devotion to Mary as a vestigial remnant of paganism, can learn from *Mary, Archetype of the Church* how much is really at stake in theological discussions of the Blessed Virgin. Indeed, the book could be read with profit by Roman Catholics in America, by American Christians who are not Roman Catholics, and by Americans who are not Christian; for each group will find itself addressed and challenged, perhaps even instructed, by this essay.

For Americans generally, one of the chief contributions of Father Semmelroth's exposition is its attack upon the extremes of individualism. Whether Roman Catholic or Protestant, American Christians have frequently interpreted the Christian faith as a matter between God and "my little soul," to be cultivated by personal decision in response to evangelistic preaching or by the private pieties of the rosary and of tabernacle devotion. Partly based upon this religious heritage and partly contributing to it, American secular individualism tends to see social issues as the composite of individual moral issues, public life as merely private life writ large, and corporate entities as nothing more than the sum total of the persons who make them up. Surely the experiences of modern life and the course of modern history have done much to expose the inadequacy of such individualism, but it is necessary to recognize that the very elements of our intellectual and spiritual tradition that are usually cited in support of this notion are in fact an important resource for the recovery of the corporate understanding of human life. For example, people of widely differing religious persuasions are agreed that the faith of the Reformation was a fountainhead of individualism. All of them "fail to understand that while this faith is something utterly different from obedience to the authority of the Church, it is not an individualistic religiousness."[3] Thus a deeper understanding of the Protestant Reformation is helping to overcome the individualistic heresy in Protestantism.

In an amazingly similar way, Roman Catholic devotion to Mary both exemplifies individualism and provides a rich resource for transcending it. As this volume points out, there is an intimate link between certain forms of Marian pietism and a view of the Church as a collection of individuals. It is inevitable that in such pietism the fuller meaning not only of ecclesiology, but also of Mariology, should be lost. Therefore the patristic parallel between Eve and Mary, evident already in St. Irenaeus and probably originating in the primitive Church,[4] provides an important corrective upon both this doctrine of the Church and this view of the Blessed Virgin. For just as St. Paul's parallelism between Christ and Adam, of which the *Virgo Eva— Virgo Maria* typology is at least a corollary, rests upon a corporate understanding of Adam as Humanity and of Christ as New Humanity (with far-reaching significance for the doctrine of the Fall and of Original Sin); so the doctrine of Mary set forth in this volume is a profound illustration of how great *typoi* such as those summarized in Daniélou's *Sacramentum futuri*—and indeed, all the *typoi* of human experience and aspiration, from Abraham the patriarch to Abraham Lincoln—embody the total life of a people and are no longer private persons.[5] It is perhaps symptomatic of our need for such a corrective that many Americans would translate *typoi* here as "ideals" or even as "mere symbols."

Yet most of the readers of this volume will undoubtedly be Christians, and more likely Roman Catholics than Protestants or Orthodox. For them, too, *Mary, Archetype of the Church* should prove enlightening in both the doctrinal issues involved. As far more competent observers have pointed out repeatedly, the very history of the Church in America has often served to obscure the doctrine of the Church, and a preoccupation with bricks and mortar has sometimes crowded out the vision of the Church as the Mystical Body of Christ. Of course, the liturgical renewal of the Church, bound together as it is with a revival of the study of Sacred Scripture, is the chief way for Roman Catholics (and not only for Roman Catholics!) to learn that the Church breathes by the presence of the indwelling Spirit and that she draws her sustenance from the Bread of Life. But an essential element in any liturgical renewal within Roman Catholicism is the transformation of subjective piety into liturgical piety, e.g., the elevation of private Marian devotion to the level of participation in the *ordo* of the Church. If, as the author says, "true devotion to Christ is Marian in attitude," the converse is even more true and more necessary: true devotion to Mary, as the Creeds and the Fathers of the Church have always insisted, is Christocentric in its origin and in its character. Liturgically, this means that the Marian feasts are not a sentimentalized Catholic version of Mother's Day, but the recognition and celebration of the unique position accorded to the Second Eve in the economy of salvation, as the conclusion of this volume makes clear.

Not only will a study of this volume help to correct abuses and misunderstandings of Mariology, but it will serve to stimulate a careful reappraisal of ecclesiology. A colleague has suggested recently that the full scope of the doctrine of the Church cannot be arrived at through the exploitation of any single metaphor for the Church, not even the "Body of Christ," but must be based upon a collation of all the images for the Church—a method that was applied by Fathers like St. Athanasius to other doctrinal issues.[6] Even a theologian who cannot accept all of Father Semmelroth's presuppositions can recognize that a reformulation of the doctrine of the Church in which the archetypical character of Mary is related to other images can significantly alter one's thought and language about the relation between the Church as organization and the Church as organism. His suggestive comments, both exegetical and historical, about the identity of the Woman described in the twelfth chapter of the Apocalypse of St. John are a good illustration of the bearing that Father Semmelroth's method can have upon the doctrine of the Church. Indeed, the exegesis of the Fathers would suggest that St. Paul's allegory of the two wives of Abraham as the two covenants and therefore as the two communities of Old Israel and New Israel could be exploited even more deeply for its possible contribution to the whole question of continuity and discontinuity in the history of the Church as the people of God.

Concerned as they must be with the question of continuity and discontinuity, Protestants will also benefit from Father Semmelroth's treatise; at least this one did. The fundamental assumption with which Protestant theology must come to terms here is that neither the doctrine of the Church nor the doctrine of Christ can be fully articulated without some doctrine of Mary. In the dogmatic development of the early Church it is evident that much of the debate over the person of Our Lord was Mariological in its focus. The Docetic heresy, which denied the full reality of His human nature, was answered by a discussion of His nativity from the Virgin.[7] The Nestorian heresy, which denied the full participation of His humanity in His deity and vice versa, was answered by St. Cyril and other Fathers, and then by the Council of Ephesus in 431, by calling the Blessed Virgin *Theotokos*.[8] Christological orthodoxy, therefore, was bound up with the clarification of the role of Mary in the plan of God. Protestant theology must ask itself whether this connection between Christology and Mariology was a historical coincidence or whether there was in fact some ineluctable obligation in the orthodox confession of Jesus Christ that compelled the Church to speak as it did of His Mother. For anyone committed to the confession of the Nicene Creed, the history of Protestant Christology since the repudiation of traditional Mariology is not very reassuring. Far from being a rival to true faith in Jesus Christ, the Marian dogma of the Church has claimed to be a necessary part of the orthodox witness to Him. This claim, as synthesized in the speculations of this book, has at least enough historical warrant to deserve consideration.

But *Mary, Archetype of the Church* will be instructive for Protestants also because of its critique of the excesses of certain forms of folk piety. When such excesses are criticized by Roman Catholic theologians, one frequently hears defensive reactions from devotees of this or that special cult or shrine, with dark hints about deviationism or "Mariological minimism." But the official declarations of the Holy See and sharp warnings from bishops and theologians throughout the Church are a documentation that though the patience of the Church with the extremes of popular sentimentality may be exasperatingly forbearing and even downright indulgent, it is not quite infinite. Father Semmelroth's gentle but devastating attack upon "some misconceptions" of what is meant by "Mary as coredeemer" is proof that Roman Catholic theology and churchmanship can and will draw a line beyond which Marian devotion and Mariological speculation must not be permitted to go. And although Protestants would certainly wish that the line had been drawn closer and sooner, they need to be reminded that such a line has in fact been drawn, and that the basic religious motivation for drawing it is in fact an evangelical one. Meanwhile, Protestant theologians and churchmen will have to give more responsible attention to the question of what they propose to do about deepening and purifying the popular religion of their own members.

The current vogue of the phrase "separated brethren" may blunt the sense of loss it is intended to voice; recognition that the walls of our separation do not reach to heaven may reduce the urgency of doing something about the walls here on earth. It only takes the study of a book like this to revive the urgency. There is something so *simpático* and yet so alien, so heartening and yet so repelling, about both the thought and the language of such a treatise that both the word "separated" and the word "brethren" begin to speak with a new poignancy across the walls. There still remains the scandal that brethren who have God as their Father and Christ as their Elder Brother should be as separated as they are in their attitudes toward Mary as the Mother of God.

Yale University   JAROSLAV PELIKAN
                                 Titus Street Professor
                                 of Ecclesiastical History

NOTES

1. George D. Smith, *Mary's Part in Our Redemption* (New York, 1938); Juniper Carol (ed.), *Mariology* (3 vols.; Milwaukee, 1955 ff.); Jaroslav Pelikan, "Mary the Mother of Jesus," *Encyclopaedia Britannica* (1963 printing), XIV, 996–998; *idem*, *The Riddle of Roman Catholicism* (New York, 1959), pp. 128–142.

2. Yves Congar, *Christ, Our Lady, and the Church*, tr. by Henry St. John (London, 1957).

3. Wilhelm Pauck, *The Heritage of the Reformation* (2nd ed.; Glencoe, Ill.: Free Press, 1961), p. 6.

4. See Chapter 2 below.

5. Jean Daniélou, *From Shadows to Reality. Studies in the Biblical Typology of the Fathers*, tr. by Wulstan Hibberd (Westminster, Md., 1960).

6. Paul S. Minear, *Images of the Church in the New Testament* (Philadelphia, 1960); on St. Athanasius, cf. Jaroslav Pelikan, *The Light of the World. A Basic Image in Early Christian Thought* (New York, 1962), pp. 21–32.

7. Cf. Tertullian, *On the Flesh of Christ*, Ch. 1 ff.

8. J. H. Newman (ed.), *Select Treatises of St. Athanasius* (2nd ed.; London, 1881), II, 210–215.

Mary, Archetype of the Church

THE BASIC MARIAN IDEA

I

The Archetype of the Church

CHAPTER 1

The Controversy
over the Basic Marian Idea

The Problem Stated

The figure of Mary appears in the very early documents of Christian tradition. The Early Fathers, who defended the Church's teaching by probing the depths of its substance, were indeed aware of the mystery of Mary. It could not be otherwise. Mary is too close to the center of the mystery of salvation for the Fathers' expositions not to treat and justify her position.

There is, however, a significant and very essential difference between Mary's role in Early Christian tradition and the part she has played in later literature, particularly that of the Middle Ages and, later, in the intolerable amount of pious works produced by the piety of rationalism, with all its superanalytic and individualistic tendencies.

In the literature of Early Christianity, especially in the apologists of the second century, Mary is not the object of any particular devotion; she is the representative of a theological idea. The mystery of the divine economy of salvation is both enclosed and expressed within her. In these early writings she emerges, not as a figure venerated through the practice of a devotion, but as an object of theo-

logical speculation. Niessen, speaking of the entire Early
Christian period up to the fourth century, says: "Dogmatic
treatments of Mary are to be found but there are no proofs
indicating public veneration."[1] Proof is lacking because official veneration of the saints did not exist at that time.
When martyrs and confessors eventually became objects of
veneration and supplication, Mary was even less in evidence. "Direct public veneration of the Virgin, even in the
fourth century, lagged behind the veneration given to other
saints. . . . In St. Jerome's time there was not a single feast of
Mary and there was perhaps only one Church called the
Church of the Blessed Virgin."[2]

This is far from saying that Mary had no significance in
the Christian thought of the Early Church. Ignatius of
Antioch, Justin, Irenaeus, and Tertullian are eloquent wit-
nesses to the contrary. Mary's importance was simply of a
different modality than in later periods. Her importance,
one might say, was theological. The Early Fathers saw her
as a Second Eve. They saw that she filled this role in a way
that was basic—not accidental—and they unveiled the mystery of salvation that shone through her. They may have
venerated her personally, just as they venerated Christ, who
redeemed the guilt contracted by Adam. But poetic hymns
of praise and the fervent prayers to Mary come at a later
time.

The Marian piety of our own age is in sharpest contrast
to the ideas we have just reviewed. Beginning in the Middle
Ages, piety underwent a change on the personal, subjective
level. Isolated and individualistic elements pushed to the
fore. With the passage of time a distinctly one-sided development took place. The Marian piety of the West be-

came more and more a matter of personal devotion, a tender love of heart speaking to heart. The sensitivity for the real totality and oneness of the Church was increasingly lost, and lost with it was the idea of Mary as the representative of the Church. Her veneration is no longer based on the redemptive idea that a part of the very mechanism of salvation is enclosed within her. Rather, the basis for her veneration is simply the personal, moral contact that unites her with her Son. The physical oneness of her motherhood is not under question, but what now makes her the object of special veneration is simply her contribution as a person. It is her power of intercession that draws man to her, not the fact that the reality of the scheme of salvation found personal expression within her.

In recent decades, great progress has been made towards the rediscovery of the innermost nature of the Church. No longer is the Church a mere congregation of many redeemed persons. She never was, of course, even though she was considered so for a long time in Western thought. In our day we are again seeing the Church in her supernatural organic unity as the Mystical Body of Christ. We are members of this Body and because of this fact we are redeemed. The opposite is not true: that is, we cannot claim that the community of the Church is gathered together from the many who have been redeemed.

The Church, newly awakened to an awareness of her true nature, venerates Mary. Thus, simultaneously with the renewal of the Church's inner vitality, a Marian movement is underway. Unfortunately, however, simultaneity does not always mean inner connection, at least not in the minds of those who represent these movements. What the

Marian movement of our day seeks is a deeper penetration
and recognition of truths felt to be essential, truths sought
from deeper understanding of the nature of revelation, or
even of the truths revealed.

Mary is no longer looked upon only as the object of special devotion; nor as the one to whom urgent prayer of intercession is to be directed. Rather, she is sought at the very
center of the work of salvation. When we see her there,
our veneration will be filled with interior vitality and
strength. At the same time it will be based on an ontological
reality established by God and asserted by man when he
venerates her. Thus, the characteristics of Mariology of
Early Christian times (namely, Mary as representative of
the mystery of salvation and consequently the object of
theological speculation) would be united with those which
later generations have accepted as their own Marian habits.
The earlier concept would be united to personal veneration,
love, and prayers for her intercession. The result would be
a theological grasp of Mary's position within the plan of
salvation, from which, despite its sober objectivity, would
flow a strong and vital piety. This piety would affirm
Mary's position and the mystery of salvation personified
within her; at the same time it would be a Marian devotion
based on reality.

To explore the possibilities of this, however, it is impossible for Mariology to line up the individual mysteries of
Mary, one by one, and enjoy each for itself. Such an approach renders them powerless and without appeal. Beauty
does not consist in individual values but in the harmony of
the whole. Mariology, to achieve proper Marian piety,
needs the illumination of its own interior values. But these

values can be seen only if the entire cluster of values is il-
lumined at the point of their interlocking inner significance.
Mariology lacks this illumination more than any other theological field. Even though the deeper meaning of the individual mysteries has been grasped, the overall illuminating
vision is still missing; there is still no definite clarity regarding the basic Marian principle. Even the bridal aspect of divine motherhood, proposed by Scheeben[3] and Feckes[4] as
the fundamental principle explaining all others, will not
yield the ultimate meaning of all Mariology. It does not
penetrate sufficiently into the mystery of salvation. We will
have more to say on this later. As long as we ask the question "Why has God made Mary the bridal Mother of
God?" and give our answer within the framework of Mariology itself, we have not yet found the basic principle, because this answer does not bring us close enough to the center of the history of salvation.

The mystery of Mary received its inner unity when God
established it. The re-presentation of this inner unity is the
task of theology. We are vitally aware that all Marian theology has to be formed from a single principle which governs the whole. Theological developments in general, however, have tended to treat Mariology as a tract by itself,
independent of the others. (This was not always the case,
and there have been exceptions in the more recent past[5] and
in the present.[6]) The tendency to divide Mariology into
individual sections and to include them within correspond-
ing tracts on Christology and grace makes good sense; it
could well shed light on Mary's essential position in the
plan of salvation. On the other hand, the methodology
which treats Mary within an individual tract also has ad-

vantages. The only basic requirement here is to be certain how to incorporate correctly a complete tract of this sort into the general theological synthesis.

Theological speculation is the spiritual re-presentation of a reality ordered by God's eternal Wisdom. It is the retracing of the principle of order ruling the divine order of salvation. That is why Mariology must emerge as if it were a single tract within the scope of theological study. In other words, within the economy of salvation Mariology has to have a place awarded to it, dictated by the specific position and function of the subject which it treats. Thus, the question arises: how can Mary be treated most objectively? In answering, one must ponder whether her function in the scheme of salvation would find a clearer expression if illuminated at each crucial point of the divine-human scheme of things; or, on the other hand, if her role is of such singular unity and central importance that it seems to make her the individual object of a theological treatise. As we consider this question, we note that Mariology is in the same situation as was the theology of the Church, which for years could not claim a tract of its own. When a tract was finally achieved the essential position and mission of the Church was still not adequately expressed. But today we know that the Church in its supernatural entity is entitled to its own dogmatic tract, based on its essential function in the process of salvation. This tract should be placed between Christology and the teachings on grace, exactly where the doctrine of Mary is generally treated today.

Does this mean that Mariology should be looked on as a usurper, preventing an essential part of theology from occupying its rightful place? Or does the substance of both tracts possibly justify their occupying the same level? In answering these questions, we must examine the content of both tracts. To express the problem more exactly, the fundamental ideas of both tracts must be compared. The divine idea that vivifies Mary and totally governs her concrete existence must show her to us as the figure standing, in her role as Mediator, between Christ and grace. The Church must be similarly considered. It is immediately clear that the divine idea is realized in the Church and that the Church functions for man's redemption according to the pattern of this idea. With this comparison made, it may possibly be proved that the idea underlying both the concept of Mary and the concept of the Church is the same. Their similar roles in the work of salvation might possibly cause them to be the parallel objects of theological investigation.

If we wish to treat Mary in a theological fashion, we must try not only to investigate the mere fact of her existence. We must also investigate the reasons for her existence, and this brings us into the study of her position as related to the entire synthesis of theology. The object of theology in general is certainly not something static; rather, it is a dynamic presentation of the economy of salvation, a continual sanctification. Therefore we must examine not only the particular parts of this process in their individual existence; we should also go back and forth from one part to another, seeking to plumb the deeper reason of each. We must ask ourselves why and how such a thing is so and not otherwise. Of course, in such investigation the theologian must be guided by a certain reverence which is ready, under some circumstances, to throw all further progress upon God's positive Will and give up any further explanations.

Yet it would not be reverent to wish to abandon the quest
from the outset simply because we are overwhelmed by the
Divine Omnipotence. The end result of such theological
positivism is to make God look like a whimsical player or
irrational tyrant, since at each juncture of revelation this
method cites God's Will as the only and ultimate explanation of everything. Actually, what God's Will creates was
first planned by His Intellect, revealing His individual mysteries to us in such a way that we seek the connecting links
binding the many individual parts into a harmonious whole.
The links are there to be found and God does not create
according to whimsy; He creates according to an inner
meaningfulness. His revelation to us is imparted to a living,
active mind made in His image. The very fact that our
minds meditate upon God's revelation gives honor to Him
as the God of revelation. A mere recording of the words of
God's revelation of which we are absolutely certain is as
little reverent as the hiding of the talent for which the passive, fearsome servant was so severely rebuked.

What we have said implies nothing more than that the
theologian discovers, among the individual parts of the history of salvation which he is treating, the unifying ground-
principle of the part upon which he is presently working.
He then binds this to the ground-principles of other parts
and so brings about a higher unity. Reigning supremely
above all—uniting and integrating all—is the final and supreme idea of God, the all-embracing *Eidos*, the one which
embraces the meaningful multiplicity of creation and the
economy of salvation.

Thus, it can be seen precisely why Marian theology
leaves us so unsatisfied, despite all the effort, despite all the

religious affirmation of which man is capable. Marian theology lays bare a disappointing inadequacy in all Marian piety, even the most legitimate. The inadequacy has its root in this dilemma: On the one hand, the presence of Marian devotion and religious feeling at the center of the Church's life obviously spurs one to ask for the inner meaning, for the significance of the reality which God created in Mary. The question is pressing because man intuits that there must be a reason for it. On the other hand, when we turn to theology, which is supposed to raise an intuition into the light of conscious clarity, we are disillusioned in finding how little the question has been answered. Mariology itself offers even less explanation than do other theological tracts.

It is not surprising therefore to find in our generation an eager search for the basic principle of Mariology. It is the search for the principle which can gather the individual mysteries into a meaningful unity; a principle which, as the starting point of every other related consideration, can form the root linking this tract to the higher synthesis of all other theology. This principle cannot of course be determined by a person fanatically pursuing theological will-o'-the-wisps. No system true to itself is whimsical. Rather, it is the representation of an existing order made by a reasoning spirit. This is very true of the situation we have under discussion. If we search for the basic principle of Marian theology, it will "have to be found as that idea which the Divine Spirit envisages and which therefore represents the root of all other individual values."[7] If we could demonstrate this principle by some truth in which Mary would be placed in the center of the economy of salvation, then we would understand why "the humble Virgin of Nazareth, who apparently only serves as the object of the heart's yearning and of pious veneration (and not as an object of scientific thought), has become the theme which, more than any other, has occupied the Christian mind."[8]

The Search for the Basic Marian Idea

The deliberate, conscious search for the fundamental Mariological principle has been and is the product of modern times. This does not mean that there had been no previous search in earlier Mariological study. But the older effort was not really a search. It was, understandably, a linking of all facets of Mariology to the one which today is the starting point and logical principle of most tracts on the subject—namely, the motherhood of God. Feckes felt compelled to state: "Any development of a Mariology whose fundamental principle is not the divine motherhood would violate the direction sanctioned by all tradition."[9]

It cannot be denied that the motherhood of God is very much in the forefront of Mary's veneration by the faithful. Any fundamental Marian principle which would mitigate this dignity or remove it from its central position would bear the seal of fallacy. The Encyclical *Fulgens Corona*, in which Pius XII proclaimed the Marian year of 1954, affirms this point.[10] Yet it is easy to demonstrate that Mary's divine motherhood, as understood by Irenaeus and Justin, for example, occupied a different position in theological thought than it did in the mind of Suarez (to use a random comparison) when he wrote: "The dignity of the Mother of God is compared to other created graces as the First Form is to its properties; conversely, the other graces must be compared to it as properties to a form.[11]

The Early Fathers when speaking of Mary praise the Virgin because she gave her *fiat* to the message of the angel and accepted what God planned to accomplish through her. Justin makes the following comparison: "Eve, an undefiled virgin, conceived the word of the serpent and brought forth disobedience and death. But the Virgin Mary replied to the Angel Gabriel's good tidings with joy and belief. The Spirit of the Lord would come upon her and the Power of the Almighty would overshadow her; accordingly the Holy One who was to be born of her would be God's Son. She said, 'Be it done to me according to Thy Word.' "[12] Irenaeus is noted for his juxtaposition of Eve and Mary: "Just as the virgin Eve had Adam for a husband . . . became disobedient and caused her death and that of all humanity, so the Virgin Mary had a predestined husband, remained obedient and caused salvation for herself and the whole human race."[13]

This very act by which Mary became the Mother of God is the reason why the Early Fathers used her as the object of their theology. In their very praise of her they brought her obedience into juxtaposition with Eve's destructive disobedience. We will explain later in what sense Mary's obedience was salvific. Suffice it to stress at this point that within this juxtaposition is found the principle which raises Mary to the sphere of theological speculation. Thus, it would seem after all that the divine motherhood is the basic principle of the Mariology of these Early Fathers, would it not?

It is precisely here, however, that a problem arises: How can one mystery serve as a fundamental principle while at the same time touching upon another mystery which lacks any inner, logical connection with the first? How can one mystery elucidate another that is in contrast to it? The Virgin Mary is contrasted to Eve. But this virginity appears in no way to draw its explanation or propriety from the motherhood of God.

If divine motherhood enters the picture when praise is first given to Mary, it does so only in the sense that this very mystery is considered the first and probably the most important step towards the understanding of the idea that first envelops her—the idea of the Second Eve. Mary has a definite place in God's idea for man's sanctification, and this place is pointed out for her by the parallel with Eve. When Mary became the Mother of God by saying her *fiat*, the first stage of this idea became realized. Thus the divine motherhood, as such, is not the principle of Mariology. According to the Early Fathers, the origin of the principle obviously lies in an overall idea in the mind of God.

If it is thought that the divine motherhood takes priority in Mariology in the Fathers' first testimony (Justin, Irenaeus, and Tertullian), this could only be a motherhood specified by another principle. But this would signify a duality which would have to be traced back to a higher unity, for a fundamental idea, as such, can be one only. Whenever a fundamental idea breaks up into a duality, it loses its fundamental note and enters the world of multiplicity. We will see that the search for the fundamental Mariological principle finally ended in its historical development at the point where it started, that is, with the Early Fathers.

When Nestorius shaped his Christological heresy in a Mariological formula, the truth about Mary's divine motherhood came to the fore. Indeed the truth had always been believed, and prior to this time it had been formulated in the word *Theotokos*. From the time of the Council of Ephesus, in fact, the divine motherhood was a fundamental principle of Mariology. Since that time all Mariology sounds like a variation of Cyril of Alexandria's praise of Mary, which he included in his great tract against Nestorius. He speaks of "the venerable treasure of the entire universe." He greets her first of all as "the bearer of God."[14] As a result she appears as "the vanquisher of all heresies in the entire world."[15] Because she stands, as mother, so close to the God-man, all attacks directed against the Redeemer must necessarily touch her too. And the victorious clarification of Christ's position as God-man was expressly formulated by the phrase, "Mother of God." It is no wonder that from then on people believed they had found access to the innermost mystery of Mary. At that time the search for a further foundation—a search that moved even Augustine to speculate on the divine motherhood as fundamental—waned more and more. "Augustine, however, was not content to recognize this teaching as ultimate. He searched for a much deeper reason for the divine birth and his speculation sought to answer the question: Why did Christ want to be born of woman?"[16] Nevertheless, the divine motherhood was increasingly held to be a self-sufficient fundamental mystery, and questions as to its further meaning were henceforth neglected.

The mystery of divine motherhood has thus gained a commanding place within Marian theology. Mary's dignity as the Mother of God became the dominating principle which governed Mariology in Scholasticism. But when one

investigates the derivation of all other Marian mysteries
from this one (which Feckes calls "the supreme idea of the
Catholic concept of Mary"[17]), one is apt to find facile rea-
sonings which cannot conceal a certain speciousness and
superficiality. The expected organic growth of one mystery
from the other is lacking. The dominating major term no
longer sounds very scientific when it proclaims: "It is fitting
that the like of this Virgin, who shone in such purity, could
not be found under God."[18] Or Bernard's words: "It cannot
be presumed that what few mortals have received should
justly be denied to this great Virgin."[19] Outlandish principles can be derived from such rhetoric—a point amply
proved by the theology and piety based on them. The reason is precisely this: a principle was established here as ultimate even though its origin continued to lie hidden within,
like a soul within a body.

It is thus evident that the purely physical entity of divine
motherhood cannot be the prime principle without under-
going some further specification. A more exact limitation
was given to this principle, which led finally to the term
"adequate motherhood of God." But by assimilating (*ade-
quare*) the divine motherhood with the other positions
which Mary holds in the economy of salvation, open ad-
mission was made that the mere fact of divine motherhood
was insufficient as a fundamental principle.

Finally, the "adequate motherhood of God" becomes almost tautological as Lépicier defines it: "The divine motherhood must be considered as adequate, that is, it must be
considered as the totality of graces and gifts proper to the
dignity of the Mother of God according to God's plan."[20]

Lépicier's "adequate motherhood" is Mariology in its entirety, not its fundamental principle.

The end result is not very different if one adduces an historical point of view in this argument in place of the logical; for example, if one were to follow Bover one would claim that the divine motherhood as such is inadequate, but when seen historically becomes sufficient.[21] But this, after all, is precisely what we are seeking—the idea God had in mind which explains and intelligibly proves the historical fact of the divine motherhood.

Scheeben and Feckes seem to come much closer to the essential truth, when, desiring to make the divine motherhood a root principle of Mariology, they specify it with a bridal nature. "Mary is a mother because she is a bride and a helpmate. This means that as *adjutorium sibi simile* she is to contribute everything in the total plan of redemption that can possibly be assigned to her. Heading the list is her making the Incarnation possible through her role as a mother. Mary is a bride because she is a mother, or because her role as mother, made possible by her *fiat*, is bridal in character."[22] Scheeben calls this Mary's "personal characteristic."[23] Scheuth sees the adequacy of divine motherhood in the fact that Mary became the bridal mother of God by her free consent; thereby he also proclaims it as the fundamental principle.[24] In another part of his book, however, he emphasizes the bridal element to such an extent that the divine motherhood seems, not fundamental, but derived from some other mystery. "Historically considered, the bridal element is the first and real principle of the entire Catholic Mariology This is true both logically and speculatively; it alone virtually contains the entire Catholic teaching on Mary and thus forms the foundation of dogmatic development."[25]

We have now arrived at the point where recent research has tried to overcome the undeniable duality implied by "bridal motherhood," by joining the two concepts into one "higher" idea unifying both. The necessity here, however, is not so much one of discovery as re-discovery. This is so because the concept of bridal motherhood, propounded by Scheeben as Mary's personal characteristic, is already contained in the primitive Christian idea of Mary as the Second Eve. It is here that the foundation of both elements, namely brideship towards Christ, really appears as primary. We note that Scheeben himself depicts Mary as the Second Eve. And Deneffe, in a lecture to the Marian Congress in Tongerloo in 1937, attempted to avoid the duality inherent in the idea of the Second Eve which Scheeben and Feckes had established as the fundamental principle.[26] Feckes himself admitted this duality when he said: "The individual Marian teachings can be proved only by relying in part on the idea of maternity, by relying in part on the idea of Eve. Only the inner unification of both aspects can satisfy the demands for an organic development of Mariology."[27] Feckes' suggestion "that both seemingly disparate ideas should be united (because of their inner solidarity in Mary) into one single divine idea"[28] is something that other authors will have to complete in their grapplings with the concept of the Second Eve. Smith recently said: "Essentially the entire doctrine of Mary's part in our redemption is contained implicitly in the statement: Just as Christ is the Second Adam, Mary is the Second Eve."[29]

Thus it would appear that this lengthy theological development has swung full circle to its starting point. Is this a case of retrogression where progression should have been expected? Certainly not. Within the fertile soil of the Church's tradition and through her theological investigation, the revealed knowledge centered in this concept has unfolded into a large and rich multiplicity. This is so even though individual considerations have for some time caused the fundamental unifying idea of God's constructive power to be forgotten. The end result of the type of development we have outlined may well be that this dynamic life-power will be rediscovered once more, and will integrate multiplicity into the one idea from which it sprang. That idea will be the same as at the beginning: Mary the Second Eve, the Mother of all the living. In our day, however, the stressing of this idea will give Mariology a content abundantly vital, yet different from that of the primitive days of its development. Yet, what Livius wrote in connection with his patristic investigations will still hold true: "There is really no objection to presuming that knowledge of revealed truth in the early Church (though less articulate) was better than that of later theologians."[30] "From Justin to Gregory the Great, all the Fathers gave such clear and overflowing praise to Mary that future generations were bound to repeat their words and be their echo."[31]

Thus, the idea of the Second Eve stands behind the mystery of Mary as its foundation principle. But we must insist that even this will not satisfy us if we wish to seek out that principle in the economy of salvation which gives to Mary a God-given and clearly revealed position. The fact that Mary is the Second Eve is, after all, a picturesque wording of an idea which it is our present task to elucidate. There must be a mystery of salvation enclosed within Mary which we should find by traveling the parallel routes suggested by the comparison of Eve and Mary. Actually, the Fathers' own words show us which mystery of God's plan of salvation was figured in Mary: It is the *Ecclesia* which shines forth in Mary, the center of God's plan of salvation, the economy of salvation in its concrete form.

NOTES

1. *Die Mariologie des hl. Hieronymus, ihre Quellen und ihre Kritik* (Muenchen, 1913), p. 198.
2. *Op. cit.*, p. 199.
3. *Dogmatik* III, n. 1587ff.
4. "Das Fundamentalprinzip der Mariologie," in: *Scientia sacra*. Festschrift fuer Kard. Schulte (Koeln-Duesseldorf, 1935).
5. Scheeben, *Dogmatik* III.
6. Schmaus, M., *Katholische Dogmatik* II (Muenchen, 1949).
7. Feckes, C., "Das Fundamentalprinzip der Mariologie," p. 258.
8. Morgott, F., *Die Mariologie des hl. Thomas von Aquin* (Freiburg, i.B. 1878), I.
9. "Das Fundamentalprinzip der Mariologie," p. 266.
10. *Acta Ap. Sed.* 45 (1953), p. 580.
11. *De incarnatione*, q.27, displ., sect.2.
12. *Dialogus cum Tryphone Judaeo* 100. – MG 6, 712 A.
13. *Adversus haereses* III, 22,4. – MG 7, 959 A.
14. MG 77, 993 B.
15. *Commune festorum B.M.V.* . . . , 3.Noct.
16. Friedrich, Ph., *Die Mariologie des hl. Augustinus* (Koeln, 1907), p. 239.
17. *Das Mysterium der hl. Kirche* (Paderborn, 1935), p. 265.
18. Anselm, *De conceptu virginali* 18. – ML 158, 415 A.
19. *Epist.* 174. – ML 182, 334 C.
20. *Tractatus de B. Virgine Maria Matre Dei* (Paris, 1901), p. 63.

21. *Sintesis organica de la Mariologia en función de la associación de Maria a la obra redentora de Jesu Cristo* (Madrid, 1929), p. 11.
22. Feckes, C., "Das Fundamentalprinzip der Mariologie," p. 269.
23. *Dogmatik* III, n. 1587.
24. Schueth, F. H., *Mediatrix. Eine mariologische Frage* (Innsbruck, 1925), pp. 75ff.
25. *Op. cit.*, p. 74,
26. This lecture is only available to me at the present in the form of a manuscript.
27. "Das Fundamentalprinzip der Mariologie," p. 272.
28. *Op. cit.*, p. 268.
29. Smith, George D., *Mary's Part in Our Redemption* (New York, Kenedy, 1938), and translated by B. Erasmi, *Die Stellung Mariens im Erloesungswerk Christi* (Paderborn, 1947, p. 67).
30. Livius, Th., *Die allerseligste Jungfrau bei den Vaetern der ersten sechs Jahrhunderte.* Uebersetzt von Ph. Prinz von Arenberg und H. Dhon (Trier, 1901), p. 51. Eng., trans., *Blessed Virgin in the Fathers of the First Six Centuries* (New York, Benziger, 1893).
31. *Op. cit.*, XXII.

CHAPTER 2

Mary, the Archetype of the Church, or the Basic Marian Idea

The Concept of Archetype

St. Ambrose said: "Mary is the type of the Church."[1] This tersely sums up what the Church had been saying from the time that Mary was first compared to Eve. It sums up the entire tradition of the Fathers and theologians concerning the Church's knowledge of its own nature. It sums up whatever continues to be expressed—at least vaguely— in almost all Mariological tracts of the present day. Ambrose saw his statement as a justifiable foundation for all pronouncements on Mary with reference to the Church. With his statement, a primitive Christian doctrine found formal expression. This doctrine is primitively Christian in a double sense: first, because it was already in existence in the early days of Christianity; second, because it belongs to the innermost and essential substance of Christian reality. It is almost astonishing that dogmatic theology did not pursue this doctrine more profoundly. We say astonishing, because the idea here is not simply an interesting comparison, but the fulfillment of the basic concern of Marian theology —the search for the fundamental principle by which Mariology finds its unity and its meaningful foundation, and through which it is seen in its proper place in God's plan of salvation.

Our primary concern in this chapter is not only the concept of type in itself, although this concept, taken in its fullest sense, contains precisely the elements that distinguish Mary's relationship to the Church and is, therefore, the most suitable instrument for the interpretation of this relationship. However, we will have to use the fullest sense of the concept in a way that is rather rare. We will not hope to derive the fundamental principle of Mariology solely from an etymological analysis of the concept of type, although we shall certainly employ this analysis. However, we must turn to ecclesiastical tradition for information concerning Mary's relationship to the Church. We will then discover that the concept of type, in its fullest sense, fits in precisely with what we have found in tradition.

When we refer to the primitive etymological meaning of type, we find an element that will prove essential in the typical relationship of Mary to the Church. A type is the effect of *tuptein*, which means a hitting or pushing. Type is originally the blow itself, and thus the primordial physical relation of one thing to another. Later, whether taken materially or abstractly, type represents only the result of the blow, an impacted image or likeness. But we are wise not to forget the primitive physical relationship upon which the concept of archetype-image is based. Indeed, in the theology of Mary, where the concept of type is fully realized, this relationship must be firmly maintained.

Type had already lost its primitive meaning in Biblical literature. The word was no longer used in the New Testament in the sense of a blow or a push. But various semantic transferrals or derived meanings can be found. For example, the word is found to mean image or shape, or the result of a beating or pushing; Thomas stated his conditions for accepting the Resurrection as follows: "Unless I see the print of the nails in His hands (*ton tupon ton elon*), I will not believe."[2] Similarly, Stephen declared in his great discourse that God abandoned the Jews to their plight because they took images (*tous tupous*) which they themselves had made and prayed to them.[3]

The transformation of the original physical idea to the abstract is more frequent in the Bible. Here type is found in the sense of content or inner fibre. For example, Paul speaks of type in the context of *tupos didakes*.[4] In the New Testament, the word also appears in the sense of archetype, both in the ontological as well as in the moral order. For example, Adam is called the type of the future Adam, Christ.[5] And the New Testament, with its continuing appeal through revelations and pronouncements to mankind, speaks with understandable preference for type in the sense of moral example. The bishops that Paul installed were supposed to be types of the faithful.[6]

The essential content of type can be threefold if taken in its fullest sense. First, it can mean the personification or representation of a spiritual entity through some sort of image. Secondly, it can mean a real bond between one entity and another as the objective foundation of this relationship. And finally, it can be a moral example as a result of this relationship. We will apply the German word *Urbild* ("very old, or original, picture"—or archetype) in a similar sense, if we conceive of type according to the meaning it implied in the Early Christian tradition. In this context, Neo-Platonism exerted an influence on the Fathers, as can be seen in their free use of the archetype-image relationship when they reflected on supernatural, grace-imbued reality. They did so rightly because the Neo-Platonic concept of the image anticipated philosophically what was fully realized in the realm of grace, namely the existence of a very real contact and some sort of causal relationship between the archetype and the image. One finds type referred to in this sense constantly by the Early Fathers, as in Justin, for example. These references are frequently similar, and are in a sense characteristic of the Neo-Platonic way of thinking (*semeion, symbolon, omoioma, parabole, mysterion*).[7]

The *first* element of the archetype concept to be found in Mariological reality is the manifestation of an idea or spiritual entity through tangible form. This kind of representation is basic in satisfying the yearnings of the human soul. The entity represented is supposed to motivate man. On the other hand, distance means some loss of the image's effectiveness. This is true whether the distance be temporal, as was the case of the figure of the Messias as seen by the faithful of the Old Testament, or whether the distance is local, as when a distant friend is brought to mind by his picture. The same is true if the distance is measured by the proportions of the reality being considered: for example, the "idea" of one's native land, or of a spiritual reality like the Church, which has a divine life-force acting behind all that appears on the surface.

Because of this factor of "distance," the object in question must be made "present." But it is impossible to bring the object (in the philosophic sense of immediacy) into close view and proximity. That is why a type must represent it, must stand in its place. Thus, the reality of the Church needs a typical representative figure, even though she is so close to us that it is in her that we live and breathe and have our being. The Church is even physically visible—and at times we are aware of her all-too-human proximity. Yet she is also remote because in her visible form we cannot touch her inmost reality. What we see and experience in her visible existence is fragmented. Both her invisible, spiritual core and the totality of her external unity call for a type to personify her and make her present to us.

Thus it should be evident why ecclesiastical tradition from early times relied upon Mary to personify the Church. In fact, this was not so much a utilization of Mary as a symbol as it was a rediscovery of the Church's characteristic features within her. It is here that we come to the *second* essential element in the concept of type which we find fully realized in Mary's relation to the Church. But the relationship of archetype and image is not founded here in the imaginative thought of the human mind, which is prone to invent a personifying figure—as, for example, the image of justice which we equip with blindfold, scales and sword. Nor is the relationship based on the chance likeness of one object to another that could leave the pondering mind suspended between the two. No, the similarity between Mary and the Church is the consequence of a very real, inner connection. The features that make the archetype similar to the image have somehow grown from the archetype into the image.

In early tradition type, *symbolon*, and *mysterion* were nearly synonymous. We can readily see why if we think a bit more about the concept of type. The object symbolized is somehow present in the symbol. Objects that can be experienced by the senses are the symbols of a divine idea, which, as their *logos* (word), is present in them. The relationship is even stronger in the case of the *mysterion* of the Church's sacramental life, wherein the believing participant-spectators come in contact with the supernatural fact of salvation, now a reality within the visible mysteries.[8]

Finally, flowing from the preceding concepts there is the *third* element: the moral example furnished by the archetype for the image. The archetype is a living person. The image is a complete entity which yet has no individual personality of its own because it is composed of various personalities who do not lose their identity in spite of the great reality of their oneness in the Mystical Body of Christ. Thus, the archetype has to be the moral example in personal attitude and subsequent actions for the members of the image.

Devotion to Mary when guided by rationalism tends to venerate her only as a model for human behavior. Great delight is taken in listing the Marian virtues; this is done upon no other foundation than the general rule that such virtues are part of the general concept of holiness. They all have to be attributed to Mary simply because she is the holiest person imaginable. There is nothing erroneous in the idea that Mary is a moral example for a Christian. The error lies only in arbitrarily using such an ethically orientated Marian piety as a means for "educating mankind" without first basing such ethical education on a definite ontological foundation. Mary as Type, however, does imply a program for the moral attitude of the Church's members. As the Type of the Church she represents its innermost essence and her personal figuration brings the Church closer to man. The united multiplicity of the Church is contained within her, as in a seed that unfolds in the breadth of time and space—just as the title of this book contains the germ of our entire exposition. But if Mary is removed from this ontological relationship, it is hard to see how a person, of whose life we have so few details, can serve as an example for the formation of Christian life.

Every kind of existence is in effect an appeal to the moral behavior of the human being coming in contact with it. When it has been established that Mary's relation to the Church and her members is factual and ontological, there will, of necessity, be a new relationship on the moral and exemplary order. We will have to order our lives (received somehow in the Church through Mary) according to the life led by the Archetype before us. The life of grace was the supernatural life-principle abounding with special perfection in the Archetype of the Church. It caused her to act in a very special and perfect way. The fact that we know few or no details concerning Mary's life is no proof to the contrary. It is Mary's attitude that establishes her as an example for the Christian, and her attitude flows from her being rooted in God, a fact she expressed to the Angel at the Annunciation: "Behold the handmaid of the Lord." By these words a fact was both established and recognized. From this she drew the conclusion that was to mark her entire life: "Be it done unto me according to Thy Word."[9]

We will return again, of course, to these triple elements

of Mary's archetypical relation to the Church. The most important element, and also the least recognized, is the second—the relation of Mary as archetype to image—for it is here that Mary's entire reality, her position in Christ's work of salvation, is enclosed.

Mary, the Archetype of the Church, in Ecclesiastical Tradition

Before we seek to show—by a deeper penetration into the content of the typical relationship of Mary to the Church—that this relationship is the unifying principle of Mariology, we wish to demonstrate first that to regard Mary as Archetype of the Church is not an invention of fanciful speculation. Rather, the unanimity of tradition seems in some way to point directly to God's revelation. In fact, we will be able to affirm that tradition seems to have located this truth within the total economy of salvation far more explicitly and unanimously than many other mysteries now presented to us as unmistakable articles of faith.

God's direct word on this subject in Holy Scripture shines forth in the "Great Sign" of the apocalyptic woman, with a radiance that leaves no doubt as to the Marian feature.[10] Scheeben goes so far as to say: "The passage in the twelfth chapter of the Apocalypse in which the redeemed are called, after Christ, 'the rest of her offspring,' affords us a scriptural argument for Mary's motherhood of men based on her motherly act of giving birth."[11] Some may object that from the viewpoint of philology and exegesis this

meaning has no support, and that Scheeben was treating the
text from a dogmatic and synthetic point of view. Such an
interpretation of this text, however, proves precisely that
philology alone cannot serve as the tool of exegesis. It is
certainly not our intention here to promote an exaggerated,
"pneumatic" exegesis. But on the other hand, one cannot do
justice to an inspired piece of writing the first author of
which is the Holy Spirit, if the philological equipment attempts to exclude the *pneuma* instead of uniting with it in
helpful collaboration.[12] With regard to the text under consideration, the exegetes, using their scientific knowledge,
have concluded that the Marian element (although not that
alone) must be symbolized by the woman of the Apocalypse. P. Gaechter, S.J., writes:

> The characteristic feature of the majestic imagery of
> Apocalypse 12 stems from Genesis 3, 15; "the
> woman," "the dragon," "the old serpent" (v. 9), and
> their enmity. Thus the prophet links together features
> which he could have borrowed only from the story of
> Mary. That is to say, the "woman" as the physical
> giver of birth to the Messias (v. 5), perhaps even
> Herod as the one through whom the dragon lies in
> wait for the birth of the Messias so as to destroy him
> (v. 4), and the flight to Egypt (v. 46). This combina-
> tion of figurative elements, all of which point to the
> one and same feature of the "woman," prove that
> John the Evangelist had long made the association be-
> tween Mary and the Proto-Gospel. . . . It cannot be
> denied that in the figure of the woman in Apocalypse
> 12 John fused the "woman" of Genesis 3, 15 and the

ideal community, which existed from the beginning, of the Messias and Mary, His earthly mother, and the Church founded by Him. All are merged together through a variety of symbolic connections.[13]

Sickenberger tried to end the centuries-long dispute as to whether the Mariological or the ecclesiological interpretation of the feminine figure should be accepted. He attempted to prove that the woman could symbolize nothing more than God's people of the Old Testament from whom the Messias sprang.[14] In his meticulous survey of the centuries, beginning with antiquity, he could quote only one passage from Augustine. This does not prove that his thesis was erroneous. His interpretation excluded, however, all other explanations, the ecclesiastical as well as the Marian. He felt they were alien to the actual sense of the passage. It is this that makes his theory subject to objections, because in the sharpest language he rejects all interpretations which could possibly be contained in the first philological and exegetical meaning, together with any other subsidiary meanings:

> If in the effort to serve two masters and unite the ecclesiastical interpretation with the Marian, one maintains first that the woman is the image of Mary, and Mary is chosen as the figure of the Church, then a line could be drawn from the woman to Mary to the Church. A complete analogy would be provided for Mary and the Church. If only parts of the image are applicable to Mary, and others to the Church, then Mary cannot be considered the symbol of the Church.[15]

This reasoning forgets entirely that the strands of the prototype and antitype are frequently intertwined in prophetic language. In the New Testament, for example, one has only to recall Our Lord's prophecy of the destruction of Jerusalem and the end of the world. The destruction of the city is a prototype for the end of the world and there is no clear separation of the features of one element from the other. Therefore it is not surprising if the features attributed to Mary as prototype cannot be clearly separated from those applied to the Church, the antitype. St. John's Apocalypse is admittedly the extreme example of prophetic language.

It is certainly true that tradition gives priority to the ecclesiastical interpretation of the present context, even though as early as the fourth century Epiphanius interpreted the woman to mean Mary. Sickenberger's historical survey of the interpretation of the passage (*loc. cit.*) shows that the ecclesiastical and Mariological explanations are quite evenly balanced and often held simultaneously by the same author. The conviction persists, however, that the Church emerges as the intended object in this figure, even if the first literal meaning can be applied to the community of the Old Testament. It is the Church typified, however, by the figure of Mary. The Protestant Hengstenberg claims that the woman "represents the one, central community of the Old and New Testament seen in the type of the Virgin Mary."[16]

The figure of the woman of the Apocalypse invokes in the believing mind the woman standing at the beginning of the Old Covenant. Both figures were inspired by the same God. Even Drewniak's investigations cast no real doubt on the Mariological interpretation of Genesis 3, 15 which, up to the present, seemed unassailable and has been a strand running throughout the Church's tradition.[17] Nor is this interpretation something that began after the Vulgate changed the *ipse* into *ipsa*, thus making it the woman who crushed the serpent, which, if applied to Eve, would be quite meaningless. The parallel between Eve and Mary in the Fathers of the second century most probably and understandably had its starting point in the promises of the Proto-Gospel. In the literal sense, the woman who becomes the serpent's enemy is Eve; yet that same Eve could never really become an enemy of the serpent in the fullest sense of the word because she fell. Thus she is represented as fulfilled in Mary. "In the text of the prophecy, the woman is represented indirectly as mother, but also directly as the bride of her son. She appears with him and beside him as *one* principle of battle, victory, and new life, as opposed to the first two human beings."[18] Thus, precisely in the light of the "Great Sign" of the Apocalypse, Mary is seen as the type of that Church whom tradition as well as Scripture[19] proclaims to be the bride of the Savior. In this development it is not our intention to claim that the passage in Genesis gives Scriptural proof that Mary is the Archetype of the Church, independent of other theological sources. But, seen in the overall light of Revelation, the woman fulfilled the task of the first Eve and became the serpent's enemy. Precisely because of this she is the fulfillment of the type of the Church, where victory over the serpent and over death are stored up. After all, Pius IX used this passage as a biblical foundation of dogma when he issued his Dogmatic Bull, *Ineffabilis Deus*, on the Immaculate Conception.

In this development it is essential to include consideration
of the event described in John 19, 26f. Veiled by the very
natural circumstances of a son's solitude, the passage speaks
of Mary's position within the economy of salvation. It may
seem strange that the theologians both of Scholasticism and
of a later era often linked this incident to Mary's spiritual
motherhood, even though this interpretation of the passage
was apparently unknown to the Fathers after Origen. Knel-
ler explains this by saying that the passage had been abused
by the exponents of synderesis, and the Fathers accordingly
had to handle it carefully and discreetly.[21]

There are, however, definite exegetical reasons for inter-
preting the passage in its literal sense as referring to Mary's
spiritual motherhood, independent of the meanings that it
had in later theology, mysticism, and piety.[22] Terrien
demonstrates clearly that none of the many testimonies
leave the slightest doubt that the text is Marian. He adds,
"It is still true that its opponents, when compared with
others, do not amount to one per cent. In fact, only three
or four at the most can be mentioned according to my
count."[23] If this interpretation is correct, then Mary doubt-
lessly stands here as the Archetype of the Church who
makes Christ's work her own and receives the fruit of His
grace. A hallowed thought within the Church's tradition is
that the Church itself was born at the Cross, issuing from
the side of the dying Second Adam.[24] This proves at once
that Mary typifies the Church because she became a spiritual Mother at the Cross. In this development it is evident
that the word "woman" represents Mary's real vocation in
the history of salvation. It is a vocation that removes her
from all the tender, personal ties that stimulate delight when

she is addressed as Mother. At the same time it raises her to a spiritual and universal motherhood. By it she possesses the official position as the Type of that feminine figure, the mother of all men, the Church.

From the treatment of scriptural passages the next logical step is a consideration of the tradition of the Fathers. In fact, the Scriptures cannot be properly understood apart from the Fathers, who took over the words of Scripture and interpreted them, aided by the "sympathy" of the divine Spirit at work in both. Tradition, above all, has carried on the comparison between Mary and Eve with the perspective upon the Church. The idea that Mary is the Type of the Church pervades the Fathers' Mariology with consistent eloquence. Accordingly, one must ask why theology has not pursued the idea more extensively, for if it had, both Ecclesiology and Mariology would have benefited greatly.

The major apologists of the second century, especially Justin, Irenaeus, and Tertullian, see the Church and its inner life in Mary. Their Mariology is based on the juxtaposition of Mary and Eve, and the viewpoint that prompts the confrontation of the two figures is precisely the one that makes Mary the Archetype of the Church. Justin writes: "Eve, an undefiled Virgin, gave birth to disobedience and death by conceiving the word of the serpent. But Mary, the Virgin, responded to the Angel Gabriel who brought her glad tidings by saying, 'Let it be done to me according to thy Word,' and she thus conceived faith and joy."[25] Mary, as God's partner, concluded a covenant of salvation between God and man. By joining in this covenant Mary became Eve's counterpart; thereby she became the Archetype of the Church and her essential task is to work out the Redemption, with Christ, in a receptive manner as His bride.

Irenaeus etched the same idea in even sharper lines. He emphasizes the idea that the Church imparts salvation by being receptive to faith. He relates this with the fact that "the Virgin Eve, bound up through her disobedience, was loosed by the faith of the Virgin Mary."[26] Here again Mary is seen clearly as the Type of the Church which mediates salvation.[27] The Church gives birth to the children of salvation enclosed in her womb in a manner prefigured by Mary. H. Koch speaks of "the *vulva*, the very womb of Mary the Mother, the image of the womb of the Church."[28] Thus, in Irenaeus' words: "Mary can joyfully sing in prophecy for the Church, 'My soul does magnify the Lord' because in Mary the *Logos* became the Son of man so that man might become the son of God."[29] The function of Mary within the history of salvation established her as the Type of the Church so firmly that words from her mouth must be understood as those of the Church.

Tertullian in turn, in his penetrating manner, shed light on the Eve-Mary-Church relationship. But he did it in a way that almost overlooked Eve. His glance passes over her to rest on the other two figures of salvation in whom Eve's mission finds its fulfillment. In Tertullian's thought, it is Mary and the Church who really became the *adjutorium* (help) to man which had been Eve's original mission. "God's same charity provided a helpmate so that nothing might be lacking, for God said it is not good for man to be alone. In doing this God knew that man would be in need of Mary's sex and later in need of the Church."[30] Thus Tertullian says, "It comes about that just as Christ was born of a Virgin we also are spiritually reborn of a Virgin cleansed of all spots through Christ. This Virgin is the Church."[31]

The second century taught this idea unanimously because it was drawn from the apostolic tradition. In succeeding centuries it became solidified in the thought of the various branches of the Church in both East and West. In Asia Minor the teaching is found expressed visibly in the inscription (circa 180–200) on the grave of Aberkios of Hierapolis in Phrygia. The inscription tells of journeys the man had made to various churches of his day. "I was able to make friends everywhere because Paul was my example. *Pistis* brought forth things from everywhere and always served us with fish, the large pure one from the spring, which a pure virgin caught." Doelger, who interpreted the "virgin" as the Church in the first volume of his *Ichthys* and as Mary in the second, would perhaps have been more correct if he had fused both concepts.[32] The Virgin is the Church prefigured by the Virgin Mary. Koch concurs in the opinion that "both concepts are present."[33]

Methodius of Olympus explicitly amplifies this tradition of Asia Minor. He does this when he teaches that it is not enough merely to proclaim the Incarnation of the Son of God through the Holy Virgin. He says: "We must also testify that the Son came into His Church as into His own flesh. Every one of us should give testimony of the *Parousia* of the *Logos* in the holy flesh taken from the pure Virgin. Every one of us should give parallel testimony to a similar coming into each of our individual spirits."[34]

The Fathers of the Alexandrian tradition also accept Mary's position as a Type of the Church. Clement, for example, identifies Mary with the Church and describes the

Church by means of features drawn from Mary. But the parallel is no coincidence, because in his development he stresses that Mary's virginal motherhood is the Archetype:

> Christ the Lord, the Virgin's Fruit, did not regard a woman's breast as blessed—in contrast to the woman of the crowd who shouted its praise. It was not He who chose it for His nourishment. Rather, because the living and good Father sprinkled the Virgin with His Word, Christ became the spiritual food for good men. One is the Father of all. One is also the Word of all. One is the Holy Spirit and He is everywhere. And also one single one is the Virgin-Mother. But I like to call her the Church. This unique Mother had no milk because she was not a woman as such. She is a virgin and a mother at the same time. She is spotless and unde-filed as a virgin. She is loving as a mother. She raises her children and feeds them with holy milk, the child-like Word.[35]

A little later another Alexandrian, Cyril, noted for his defense of the divine motherhood, identifies Mary with the Church. This is at the end of his discourse against Nestorius at the Council of Ephesus. He "praises the ever virginal Mary, namely the Holy Church, and her Son, the undefiled Bridegroom."[36]

Eloquent testimony of the Syrian tradition is found in a controversial work against the Manicheans, written by Hegemonius around 350. The work is in the form of a fic-titious conversation between Archelaus, a Catholic bishop, and the heretic Manes. Manes tries to prove that Mary is not the Mother of Jesus. He says that this position is dangerous because the Scriptures speak of Jesus' brethren. "Now answer me whether these brethren were begotten by Joseph or by the Holy Spirit. If you hold they were of the Holy Spirit, like Christ, then we have many christs. But if the brethren are not of the Holy Spirit, and you insist that Jesus had brothers, then you must positively hold that after the annunciation the most chaste Virgin and spotless Church had relations with Joseph."[37] Manes' sarcastic, bitter description of Mary as the most chaste Virgin and spotless Church must have been prompted by the prevailing Catholic thought of the time; otherwise why would this be chosen as an obvious point of debate? Migne, however, inserts the following editor's footnote: "The word *ecclesia* seems to be superfluous and added by a mistake of the copyist. Certainly the passage is understandable without it." But Ch. H. Beerson, the editor of the passage in the Berlin edition of the Church Fathers, thinks differently. He includes the word in his text.[38] And according to the rules of hermeneutics, the surprise felt at first glance should actually favor the word's being included in Hegemonius' original text.

Epiphanius of Salamis represents the Palestinian-Syrian tradition. His writings on the topic are of special significance, for they have been called "a treasure trove of literary tradition."[39] The confrontation of Eve and Mary is a familiar one to him. In the context of one of his expositions on the economy of salvation he declares; "This following biblical passage has been understood to symbolize Mary, and can be applied to the Church also: 'Wherefore a man shall leave father and mother and shall cleave to his wife and they shall be two in one flesh.' To this the Apostle adds, 'this is a great mystery. I mean in reference to Christ and to the Church.' "[40]

The Roman tradition does not rely only on Justin and Irenaeus of the second century for the idea of Mary as Type of the Church in the history of salvation. The great Fathers of the fourth century taught explicitly the doctrine which the figure of *Orante* on the walls of the catacombs and the golden glasses represented visually. The figure, in a "perspective" depiction of the soul of the buried person, represents that individual as a member of the Church prefigured by Mary. Ambrose, for example, claimed that the prophecies about Mary apply to the Church: "Those things were prophesied of Mary as image (*figura*) of the Church,"[41] It was he who first used the expression "Mary, the Type of the Church."[42]

According to Niessen: "In Jerome's writings against Jovinian there are passages from the Canticle of Canticles applied to Mary, who, as the everlasting Virgin, is the Mother of many virgins. This application converges with applications to the Church."[43]

In Augustine we find that the African tradition—to which Tertullian is witness—had reached a culmination. The idea that Mary typified the Church in her essential task of salvation occurs very often in his writings—so often, in fact, that Friedrich[44] said: "The Mary-Ecclesia parallel can be accepted without hesitation as the favorite idea of the Bishop of Hippo."[45]

In the thought of the Fathers, the bridal bond between God and man is the context wherein, above all, Mary appears as Type of the Church, the Church itself being God's

bride in the history of salvation. This prefiguration, however, does not imply that Mary is on the one hand the bride
of Christ while on the other, in a purely factual parallel,
the Church is also the bride of Christ. Rather, the Church,
through Mary as her representative, gives her bridal *fiat*
to the covenant; she assumes the redemptive work of Christ;
she receives as a bridal gift the fruits of Redemption for the
whole Church, which, in Mary, has become the Bride of
Christ. Peter Chrysologus says that the woman who
kneaded the divine Word as a leaven in the multitude of
men is both Mary and the Church.[46] In another sermon he
continues:

> God sends a winged messenger to a Virgin; his task
> is to bring back the pledge of espousal. . . . He is to re-
> ceive the *fiat*. . . . The messenger flies down quickly to
> prevent God's Bride from favoring a human espousal.
> The purpose is not to rob Joseph of his bride but to re-
> store her to Christ to whom she was pledged from the
> very beginning of her existence in her mother's
> womb.[47]

In his *Analogiae*, Isidore of Seville expertly gathered together the teaching of tradition on this subject and gave it
emphatic expression: "Mary signifies the Church who, although espoused to Christ, conceived us of the Holy Ghost
and gives birth to us as a Virgin."[48]

The Mary-Church typology continues from the patristic
period on into less brilliant literary ages. Mention must be
made of Ambrosius Autpertus of the eighth century. His
commentary on the *Apocalypse* teaches that Mary in the

figure of the apocalyptic woman "plays the role of the Church. Daily she gives birth to new generations; from her the universal body of the Mediator is being formed."[49] The next stage is the Scholastic period, and for this reference can be made to M. Grabmann's rather summary statement. He writes:

> Mary's position with regard to the idea of the Church is set forth by the theologians of the Middle Ages. They do so primarily in the light of the fact that she is included in the cluster of ideas suggested by the *Canticle of Canticles*, the high song of the *unio Christi cum Ecclesia* where the three ideas—Christ, Mary and the Church—appear in close relationship. Similarities to this kind of interpretation of the *Canticle of Canticles* are to be found in the work of Jerome and Ambrose. The interpretation itself is favored and brilliantly interpreted from the twelfth century on by Philipp von Harvengt, Algerinus von Abbatisvilla, Rupert von Deutz, Honorius of Augustodunum and Alanus ab Insulis. During the later Scholastic period it was used by Denis the Carthusian. In his authentic *Commentary on the Canticle of Canticles* St. Thomas abandons this concept. But in his explanations of Psalm 44, Aquinas clearly and intelligibly explains the very close connections between Christ, Mary and the Church. In the profound tradition of Medieval mysticism the whole idea of the Church is summed up in the word *Mary*. This is so because the love of the members for Christ, the Head and Bridegroom of the

Church, reaches its culmination in Mary's love for Christ.[50]

The bonds of history and love that connect Mary and the Church in the realm of salvation serve as foundation for the comparisons made between them in Scholasticism. We will return to this point later. It is enough to point out here that it emerges in the thought of Thomas and Bonaventure when they stress that Mary is filled with a grace called *gratia redundantiae*—a grace which overflows from her to the Church as a whole and to the individual members as well.

The emphatic teaching of early tradition found its later, ritual after-effect in the fact that so many church buildings were dedicated to Mary, for these buildings were looked upon as symbols of the Church as a whole. "Throughout the realm of the visible Church, buildings were dedicated to Mary from quite early times. They stand out as a monumental embodiment of Mary's veneration thus made visible to all eyes. Nearly all liturgists consider God's house to be the material image of Christ's Church and a symbol of Our Lord's Body. But the equivalence of Mary and Ecclesia was certainly one reason for the innumerable consecrations to Mary and at the same time served the purpose of establishing a definite place for Mary in the material realm of architecture."[51]

Just as church buildings give proof of Mary's position as Type of the Church, there existed in the Middle Ages a living architectonics which should be mentioned as witness to the convictions of the Church in that era. The Order of

St. Brigid was established in the middle of the fourteenth century. Its structure was as follows: monks and nuns were to live in separated parts of the monastery under the leadership of an abbess. The monks numbered thirteen and symbolized the College of the Apostles (including St. Paul). The nuns were sixty in number; four deacons represented the four great Latin Fathers, Ambrose, Augustine, Jerome, and Gregory; and eight lay brothers raised the number to seventy-two disciples. Thus, the entire community symbolized the universal Church. The abbess' task was to unify and direct the whole household and to serve as a symbol of Mary, the peak and point of unison, the Type of the Church.

Theology in our day cannot afford to neglect an idea which tradition brings to us as being both apostolic and revealed in origin. Parts of this idea can be found in every tract on Mariology, but they generally do not do justice to the strength which the idea has in tradition. It is in tradition that we must search for the basic principle of Mariology, for the inner meaning that orders the individual Marian mysteries in themselves and in theology as a whole. Only in this way can be explained the strength and consistency of Marian veneration in the Church.[52]

The Basic Idea of Mariology

The survey of the Church's tradition just completed should have established without doubt that Mary is the Archetype of the Church of salvation. But we are not merely concerned with this idea in itself; we must try to center this idea within the entire mystery of Mary. This involves a search for the mystery which will uncover Mariology in its entirety, simply because this very mystery is the basic idea that God wanted to fulfill in her. Thus, we must now show that Mary as Type of the Church is not a mere addition to a tract which would be complete without this mystery. Rather, this idea—the fundamental mystery itself—has to be placed at the very beginning of such a tract.

The primacy of Mary as Type of the Church can be proved by a twofold structure of thought. First of all, we can compare Mary's various mysteries with each other. By including the mystery of Mary as Archetype of the Church in that comparison, it will be found that no other idea is more basic. Secondly, we can ask ourselves which mystery most intimately unites Mary to the central point in the economy of salvation. This method is justifiable because the function of a basic principle consists both in connecting individual mysteries in an intelligible manner and in intelligibly ordering them, as an organic unity, into the entire economy of salvation. This ordering, of course, has reference to the entire body of theology, for theology is the scientific microcosm of the economy of salvation.

The mysteries of God's revelation are not a jumble of individual creations which could have been something different. They are an organism formed as a whole through an inner necessity. To put it another way, they are a part of a plan and not the result of happenstance. They show clearly that God's creative Will follows upon His planning Intellect. Thus, the task of theology cannot be the mere listing of these individual mysteries according to the words

of God's positive revelation (even though such a method
may at first seem like a kind of homage to the divine Omnipotence and Majesty which alone is responsible for the
wonders of this world and the world of grace). In reality,
such an approach would mean a lessening of the reverence
due God, because the essence of His majesty is not only the
power of His Will but the infinite wisdom of His planning
Intellect as well. In short, God's mysteries should inspire
us to adore His infinite power and give us good reason to
develop a contemplative awareness of His wisdom.

It is for this reason that Marian theology cannot be satisfied with doing nothing more than stating the privileges
with which Mary was endowed as the Mother of God. We
will be able to glorify God's wisdom and might all the more
when we recognize clearly what significance He gave Mary
and what function it is that she fulfills within the framework of His salvation.

It is much too easy to be satisfied with the statement that
Mary is God's mother. True, much of our knowledge of
her mysteries proceeds from this point, but we may and
should approach even the mystery of her motherhood with
the question: Why is Mary the mother of God in God's
plan of salvation?

While it is possible to stress the bridal aspect of the
motherhood of God, the concept can be traced back to a
more basic Marian principle. But even if such a principle
were not yet found, the question would still spring forth
from the very essence of the divine motherhood as to why
it took place at all. The fact of a human being becoming
the Mother of God is so supra-natural and supra-intelligible
that the mind is driven to examine its reason and purpose,

just as one examines the reason and purpose of the mystery of the Incarnation—*Cur Deus homo,* why did God become man? It is certain that Mary became God's mother because the *Logos* wanted to become a man among men; because He wanted to be born in a human way. Thus, the question no longer belongs to the essential Mariological sphere but to the Christological and as a result the divine motherhood seems to be the ultimate Mariological principle after all.

But the question is precisely whether or not there is another Marian mystery which serves as foundation for this divine motherhood. The basic Mariological principle is that mystery, that idea which cannot be traced back to any other in the Mariological cluster. The basic Mariological principle will be the final, logical principle for all other Mariological mysteries. If such a principle itself continues to suggest a further question, it will not necessarily be opposed to the character of a basic Mariological principle, but the answer will belong outside of the Mariological sphere.

We will now begin our search for the basic Mariological principle. Our method will be to compare with each other the Marian mysteries which have been established by the Church's doctrine. It will be evident in some cases that one is the result of another; in others, that to an extent the individual mystery can be explained by itself or at least does not rely so heavily upon another Marian doctrine, it must be reduced back to it. If we include in this comparative study the idea of Mary as Archetype of the Church, we will find the long-sought principle which serves as founda-

tion even for the bridal motherhood of God. There are no
known mysteries of Mary to which the Archetypical idea
could not be traced. We have no difficulty in stating that
because Mary is the virginal, bridal Mother of God, she is
therefore the Archetype of the Church. But we definitely
must not misunderstand the word "because" which indicates
sequence within order. Rather, we should think of the
word "because" more in terms of the conjunction "in order
that," thus stressing the essential note of sequence in the ultimate, interior order of God's Mind. This is what we are
really concerned with in our search for the basic principle,
for the idea that leads to unity. In this pattern of order the
following statement is ultimate: Because Mary was to be
the Type of the Church, she was given existence as the virginal Mother of God. There is no other Marian mystery
which, as the intentional principle, could precede and give
root to the position that Mary holds as Type of the Church.

From the reverse point of view, all other Marian mysteries draw their inner meaning and connection from this
basic mystery. The derivation of Mary's privileges (in all
the manifold variety with which they are presently studied)
is based on more or less strict convenience and their proof is
mostly a matter of personal taste and subjective viewpoint.
The dogma of Mary as Archetype of the Church, however,
helps us to see the other Marian dogmas combined into an
objective context. In the second part of this book we will
try to expound this idea, treating the individual mysteries,
and finally reaching an almost irrefutable confirmation of
what we are here trying to clarify according to the positive
tradition of the Church and the logic of the matter itself.
Psychologically the organic integration of a complete unity

will often prove the correctness of a doctrine far more effectively than a pure demonstration of proofs. But such an integration must proceed from objective necessity, for God's works are an ordered entity full of harmonious beauty. And harmony and completeness are achieved when individual components surrender to the logic of the whole and the mind is neither startled nor baffled by an element that might fall outside the unifying frame.

If we ask ourselves which, of all Marian mysteries, is the one that connects Mary most intimately with the center of salvation, we are led immediately back to the mystery of Mary as Archetype of the Church. Indeed, the only mystery which can serve as the basic principle of Mariology is the mystery that sums up the inner meaning of Mariology itself and, at the same time, forms the point by which it is rooted to theology as a whole. It is most natural to assume that the only reason for Mariology at all is Mary's close relationship to the work of salvation. The extreme importance that she has attained in Christian piety and faith shows that this relationship must be a very close one indeed.

It is equally clear and self-evident that Christ, our Incarnate Savior, is the center of the economy of salvation. Salvation is the life of the Trinity brought by Him into humanity. A favorite idea of the Patristic tradition is the following: The one great body called *mankind* was poisoned by sin, but it regained its spotlessness and its immortality through the *Logos* who came to it.

This point of view of course suggests again that Mary's divine motherhood is the basic principle of Mariology after all. What could bring Mary closer to Christ than her motherhood? Such reasoning, however, confuses again the fac-

tual connection with the intentional connection. There can
be no denial that Mary entered into the closest physical
union through her motherhood. But the question remains
as to *why* she was placed in this actual union with the God-
man.

The center of the history of salvation is not the historical
Christ in the sense in which He is treated within the mystery of the divine motherhood. The center of the economy
of salvation, its very essence, is the Whole Christ; Christ
with His Church confronting Him as His Bride, making
His work her work, receiving the fruits of His work within
her *pleroma* of grace and imparting the same fruits to the
individual members. In this union the Church is bound to
Christ in such a way that she becomes His Mystical Body,
united to Him as to her Head without any lessening of her
bridal attitude toward Him.

Thus, the basic mystery of Mariology is that which
brings Mary closer to the center of the economy of salvation, which is the Church. This coming-together, however, does not take place through the mystery of the factual
motherhood of God; rather, it takes place through the bridal
aspect of the divine motherhood, because here Mary shows
herself as the completed bridal *fiat* for the advent and work
of the Savior. This is, more or less, the essence of the mystery that we have stressed when considering Mary as the
Archetype of the Church. This mystery actually places
Mary in the center of the economy of salvation; that is to
say, in the center of the Church whose innermost essence
is the imparting of salvation. The closeness of the relationship brings about similarity of features and an inward
causal connection as well. Mary as Archetype is in closest

union with the Church because she is the germ of the Church, because she bears within herself the *pleroma* of grace that will be poured from her into the Church which unfolds in time and space. The examination of this point, the finding of the concept of type realized to its fullest in the relationship of Mary and the Church, is the further task which will be accomplished in the following pages. But this chapter can end with a word from St. Augustine who realized that the inner cause and reason of Mary's physical motherhood lies in her position as Type of the Church: "According to the flesh our Head had to be born of a Virgin through an extraordinary miracle, to show that His members, according to the Spirit, were to come forth from the virginal womb."[53]

NOTES

1. *Expos. in evgl. Luc.* II.7. – ML 15, 1555 B.
2. John 20, 25.
3. Acts, 7, 43.
4. Rom. 6, 16.
5. Rom. 5, 14.
6. E. G., Titus 4, 12.
7. Cf. de Lubac, S.J., H., "Typologie et allégorisme" in: *Recherches de science religieuse,* 34 (1947) 184, Anm. 16.
8. For the way in which the relation of Mary to the Church is ordered to the sacramental essence of the Church, cf. Semmelroth, S.J., O., *Die Kirche als Ursakrament* (Frankfurt, 1953).
9. Luke 1, 38.
10. *Apocalypse* 12.
11. *Dogmatik* III, n. 1816.
12. *Conc. Tridentinum,* sess. IV (Denzinger 783).
13. *Maria im Erdenleben* (Innsbruck, 1953), p. 226.

14. "Die Messiasmutter im 12. Kapitel der Apokalypse," in: *Theologische Quartalschrift*, 126 (1946), pp. 357–427.

15. *Loc. cit.*, p. 418.

16. *Kommentar zur Apokalypse* (Berlin, 1861).

17. *Die Marianische Deutung von Gen.* 3, 15 *in der Vaeterzeit* (Breslau, 1934).

18. Derckx, H., *Die Mutter Gottes, die Erfuellung des Weibes der Uroffenbarung* (Paderborn, 1933), p. 45.

19. Eph. 5, 21ff.

20. Cf. Grabmann, M., *Die Lehre des hl. Thomas von Aquin von der Kirche als Gotteswerk* (Regensburg, 1903), p. 302.

21. "John 19, 26–27 bei den Kirchenvaetern," in: *Zeitschrift fuer kath. Theologie*, 40 (1916), pp. 597–612.

22. Cf. Gaechter, S.J., P., *Maria im Erdenleben* (Innsbruck, 1953), pp. 201ff.

23. *La Mère de Dieu et la mère des hommes* (Paris, 1902), II, 1, pp. 247ff.

24. Cf. Tromp, S.J., S., "De nativitate ecclesiae ex Corde Jesu in Cruce," in: *Gregorianum*, 13 (1932), pp. 489ff.; also, the hymn for Vespers of the Feast of the Sacred Heart: "ex corde scisso ecclesia Christo jugata nascitur."

25. *Dial, c. Tryph. Jud.* 100. – MG 6, 712 A.

26. *Adversus haereses* III, 22,4. – MG 7, 959 B.

27. *Adv. Haer.* III, 24, 1. – MG 7, 966 B.

28. *Virgo Eva – Virgo Maria* (Berlin-Leipzig, 1937), p. 38.

29. *Adv. Haer.* III, 10, 2. – MG 7, 873 B.

30. *Adv. Marcionem* II, 4. – ML 2, 315 A.

31. Koch, H., *Virgo Eva –Virgo Maria*, p. 42.

32. *Florilegium Patristicum* III (Bonn, 1914), p. 40. – Doelger, Fr., J., *Ichthys* II. *Der heilige Fisch in den antiken Religionen und im Christentum* (Muenster, 1922), pp. 454–507.

33. *Virgo Eva – Virgo Maria*, p. 92.

34. Cf. Niessen, J., *Die Mariologie des hl. Hieronymus* (Muenster, 1913), p. 32.

35. *Paedagogus* I, 6. – MG 8, 300 B.

36. MG 77, 996 C.

37. *Acta disputationis Archelai*. MG 10, 1508 C.

38. Hegemonius, *Acta disputationis Archelai* (Leipzig, 1906), p. 81.

39. Rauschen-Altaner, *Patrologie* (Freiburg, 1931), p. 242.

40. *Haeres* 78. – MG 42, 729 CD.

41. *Expos. in evgl. Luc.* II.7. – ML 15, 1555 B.

42. *De institutione virginis* 14, 88. – ML 16, 326.

43. Niessen, J., *Die Mariologie des hl. Hieronymus* (Muenster, 1913), p. 159.

44. *Die Mariologie des hl. Augustinus* (Koeln, 1907), p. 255.

45. Cf. *Sermo* 188, ML 38, 1005; s. 191, ML 38, 1010; s. 192, ML 38, 1012; s. 195, ML 38, 1018; s. 213, ML 38, 1064; *De s. virginitate*, ML 40, 397.

46. *Sermo* 99. – ML 52, 479 AB.

47. *Sermo* 31. – ML 52, 576 A.

48. ML 83, 117 C.

49. Quoted by Sickenberger, J. *Die Messiasmutter im 12. Kapitel der Apokalypse*, p. 376.

50. *Die Lehre des hl. Thomas von Aquin von der Kirche als Gotteswerk* (Regensburg, 1903), pp. 296f.

51. Halbricht, V.G., *Maria* (Oldenburg, 1926), p. 35.

52. Reference should be made to the Proceeds of the 1951 session of the Société franç. d'Etudes Mariales, collected in: *Marie et l'Eglise* (Paris, 1953). Cf. Rahner, S.J., H., *Maria und die Kirche* (Innsbruck, 1951), and Mueller, A., *Ecclesia Maria* (Freiburg, 1951).

53. *De s. virginitate* VI, 6. – ML 40, 399.

II

Mary as Archetype of the Church That Brings Salvation

CHAPTER 3

The Co-Redeemer

THE TRADITION OF MARY as Type of the Church does not testify to a simple fact—later proved—which might have been the result of chance. Rather, tradition shows clearly that the typology points out her position within God's eternal vision of salvation. Therefore we must go beyond our present conclusions to ask *why* and *how* this mystery is so fundamental to Mariology.

We must study more exactly the substance of this typology. We must work out the aspects under which Mary typifies the Church. Therefore we will search for the innermost essence, in the economy of salvation, of both figures, Mary and the Church. Then and then only will we be able to grasp the true value shining forth from her role as Archetype. For much too long every Mariological topic has been expounded by arbitrary (if not logically ill-founded) convenience. All Mary's revealed privileges are decked around her like the crowns and strings of pearls adorning her shrines. Their value is expressed in subjective devotions, and nowhere else. They are found wanting when judged by any objective standard of beauty. Some ideas are quite astonishing. For example, one author's effort to penetrate Mary's salvific position results in this bizarre comment: "Mary's co-operation (with Christ's saving work) is nothing more than any bride's unwillingness to remain in the background; it is not an essential contribution but merely an embellishment of the great sacrifice of reconciliation."[1] This tendency to stress Christ's unique position leaves Mary's work untouched. If Mary's work is considered "embellishment," such lack of inner significance makes it no embellishment at all.

It is now our task to examine what can be said definitely about the history of salvation when we scrutinize the teaching on Mary the Archetype of the Church. We will see that Mary in truth is placed squarely as co-redeemer in the work of salvation; that she fulfills this role no differently than does the Church, the essential co-redeemer, without which Christ's work could not have its complete redemptive effect. Furthermore, we will see that Mary is the mediator of all redemptive graces imparted to men. Here again she is no different than the Church, whose function of bringing salvation was prefigured and first realized by her.

Our starting point will be the basic law governing the entire history of salvation. Our first task will be to show what is *not* implied when Mary is called co-redeemer, and here we must be careful to steer the middle course between errors of excess and defect. Certainly, the very nature of Mary as Archetype sheds light on the question of co-redemption and mediation. Koester thought that ". . . any discussion of this theological question becomes hopelessly bogged down."[2] Yet perhaps this very problem (of co-redemption and mediation) becomes elucidated by a firm grasp of Mary's typology. It may well be that this elucidation will prove more convincingly that the archetypal concept is the fundamental principle and dominating idea of the Marian mystery.

A Basic Law in the Economy of Salvation

In the theology of Christ's Redemption, there is tacit or admitted assumption that sinful man cannot save himself by his own strength alone. God had to come to man and re-establish the union disrupted by sin. What is more, reparation, the primary duty of a sinner, cannot be performed by a sinful man. Reparation is never sufficient because the essence of the situation calls for an Infinite Benefactor, who, by substitution, fills the void. Sin begins in time but its dimensions are rooted in infinity.

This doctrine is both true and basic and needs constant emphasis. Yet such emphasis must not leave the door open to the one-sided view that Redemption is only the deed of a God who gives. God's giving consists precisely in the fact that it presents man with the opportunity to be active himself. Man co-redeems because he is redeemed. The inverse of the proposition is just as true: man is redeemed because he co-redeems. "The more the Church herself is redeemed, the more she is co-redeemer."[3]

A basic law of God's redemption states that two factors operate together in salvation. (Unfortunately, in the human mind they always tend to split into "either this one or that.") Salvation means the union of God and man. This union is "transmitted" by Christ when He comes to us from the Father (*adventus*) to assume our human nature and

then returns to the Father through His sacrifice. Just as the
Incarnate Son of God wanted to be accepted by free consent, every individual endowed with God's grace is joined
in personally consummated unity with Christ as a member
of the one organism. At the same time and in the same
fashion, man preserves his own personality, and it is precisely this fact that causes his ontological union with Christ
to be transformed into a moral union. In the supernatural
realm of salvation one fact does not exclude another fact as
in the natural world. In the supernatural, man is caught up
by God into His mystical-physical oneness of Life. At the
same time, God encourages man personally to confirm and
accept everything that God offers him as His free *synergos*
(co-operator)—to use a term the Greek Fathers were fond
of.

This operation is called salvation. But even this term is
erroneous or at least does not fully express the reality. In
salvation man is to be raised to active participation in the
life-process of the Trinity. By becoming man the *Logos*
has taken possession of us human beings and united us to
Himself in a vital supernatural way. But it is through our
personal consent that we must open ourselves to receive
and then to exhale that which binds Father and Son together—the Holy Spirit.

Christ has incorporated us in Himself. By sanctifying
grace He has transformed our innermost being into His
living image. He has rooted us as His members into His
Mystical Body. This means that He has fashioned us to
Himself so much that from the earliest times ecclesiastical
tradition did not hesitate to declare that He divinized us
through His Incarnation.

The Father sees and expresses Himself in His Son; He loves this Infinite Likeness of Himself and this love finds expression in the Holy Spirit. The Son, who has this Divine Being from the Father, loves the Father and expresses this love in the same Holy Spirit. The Holy Spirit has His Divine Being only as an expression of the love in which Father and Son encounter each other. A very early tradition stated that the Holy Spirit is like the kiss of sacred love exchanged by lovers. Again, we too are rooted into this divine life. The Holy Spirit, whom the Father breathes out to the Son, also touches us who have our being in the Son. He dwells in us as the seal and pledge of the Father's love, and the Father is Father of us all because we are members of His Son. Having our being in the Son, we breathe with Him when the Son breathes out the Holy Spirit as an expression of divine love for the Father. Within us, the Holy Spirit, with ineffable groanings, calls out *Abba*, Father.[4]

This divine life can of course be given to man only by the Triune God Himself. No animal can change itself into a human being. Man is less, far less capable of performing this "divinization" by himself. It is so much a work of God's grace, that we simply call the entire process grace. In our own age the Church has again become much more aware that it is this new type of existence that makes us Christians and that all renewed Christian activity derives its value from this existence.

From another point of view, this new existence will not be correctly understood and evaluated if it is not understood as a dynamic power. The newness of Christian existence is a participation in the life of the Holy Spirit. God's nature is natural both to Him and to us who have received some part of it. Nevertheless, this participation does not eliminate the infinite distance between God and us. On the other hand it must be able to instill in us some of its infinite vitality and dynamism.

Our rooted-ness in Christ and thereby our participation in the life of the Trinity is by no means an unfolding vitality, or a blind necessity. We have been drawn into the life of the Triune God which flows among the three Infinite Persons. The reason these Persons are established in their own existence is that they each possess the Divine Life in a different manner according to the way they confront one another. The Father possesses a Divine Nature and sees it as an Image in His Son. This is what makes Him the First Person. The Son has His Being through eternal procreation from the Father. This is what makes Him Son. Thus, if the Father were to stop procreating the Son in expressing Himself, and if both were to cease breathing the Spirit in mutual love, God would be no more. The life of the Triune God is therefore a supremely personal function.

Mankind also has a part in this personality. It is a monumental fact that, even though we share the exact same nature with other human beings, we are at the same time on our own and can will to receive or reject. Our own human life, just as God's, expresses itself as an interflow of knowledge and love. But we can refuse to express ourselves. Although by uniting us to Christ He granted us participation in the life of the Trinity, God does not disturb our personal independence.

It is the *basic law of God's economy of salvation* that we can only receive divine life as a gift from God by becoming essentially incorporated into the God-man. At the same time we must make our own decision so that the union may be a bond from person to person between God and man.

The law we have just stated is evident at all stages in the work of salvation. Christ's work, which we call salvation (though to be saved from the bonds of sin represents only one element of the whole process), is not merely a moral turning toward God and His Will, stimulated by Christ's example. Neither is it only the existential unification of Divinity with mankind. It is both. And both are equally essential. Salvation, the unification of God and man, takes place first of all in Christ because He is the God-man. Christ's humanity lacks an individual personality, but in confronting the Divine Will has a very human will of its own. This will is free. Thus His work of salvation, of unification, cannot be brought about by the mere fact of the ontological union in the Incarnation. The union must be equally and simultaneously affirmed by a moral union. That is why during His life He spelled out His plan so frequently; that is why He declared that He came to fulfill the Will of Him who sent Him. This is *His* moral element and it is culminated in His death on the Cross. His sacrifice perfects the moral unification of the human and the divine.

The Church, the extension of Christ's divine, redeeming humanity, must also be the mystical-physical union of the divine and the human. At the same time it too must have a moral unification. In the fifth chapter of the letter to the Ephesians, the Church is seen in its mystical-physical union with Christ, her Head. At the same time she is seen as the Bride standing before Christ and receiving the graces of His work. Within the Church all humans who have en-

countered Christ personally, who have taken His work
upon them (and thus partake of His life through moral
union) are joined together. At the same time the Church
is the Body of Christ because her union with Him is so
close that she can be compared to the organism of a body.
Here too—in spite of the complete reality of the mystical-
physical union—the moral, personal individuality is preserved to the extent that the union is a covenant whose partners meet freely.

The granting of salvation to individual members of the
Church means that Divinity and mankind participate in a
union just as it was perfected by Christ Himself. Man's
sanctification, accordingly, must be the result of the same
basic law of the simultaneous nature of ontological and
moral union. The grace which must possess us to make us
divine does not disturb our free power of decision. The
union with Christ through the grace that incorporates us as
His members must also be moral and personal. Thus theology states that the formal effect of justification is *simultaneous*. It is both the fact of our participation in the Divine
Sonship (which fact rests on our ontological union with the
God-man) and our friendship with God, a union of two
individual personalities who discover their own being in
free surrender to each other through an exchange of recognition and love.

Consequently, it is also possible that the Beatific Vision
can be earned at the same time by a personal decision. (The
Beatific Vision is referred to as *lumen gloriae*, "the light of
glory," and is the organic unfolding of grace received in
our mortal state.)

We have seen clearly enough that salvation in its various

stages is a taking possession of man by God and man's inclusion into God's life process. But again, man possessed by God is not merely passive. Grace takes hold of him in a way that makes him remain self-reliant. He can say no; he can say yes. And he does so completely beneath the shadow of the grace of salvation so that his salvation has the nature of a dual bond between man and God. The phrasing of Revelation—to the extent that it has been received in God's written word—emphasizes this point particularly. Recurringly the Old Testament—as suggested by the very title of this book—shows that salvation through Christ was prefigured by the covenant between God and man. The stubbornness of the Chosen People, their sinful falling away, is interpreted under the figure of adultery because of the bridal bond between God and His nation.[5] In the New Testament, Christ refers to the Sacrament of the New Testament[6] in terms that stress its permanent and sacred nature. The reality of salvation permanently wears the characteristic sign of the bridal bond between Christ and His Church. "The meaning and culmination of all history is the conclusion of the covenant between man and God. Man, seen in the symbol of the bride, opens himself to God, pressing on towards Him with the longing cry: Come."[7]

It must never be forgotten, however, that the contributions to this covenant made by the two partners are essentially and infinitely distinct. Whatever the partners of the covenant have in common is bestowed exclusively by the Divine Partner. The mere possibility of the covenant is the work and gift of the Divine Partner. It would be theologically wrong and a semi-Pelagian heresy if the human partner's contribution were made to seem as though redeeming grace were given to him through a "yes" spoken without grace.

But on the other hand, man has power to refrain from concluding the covenant. When a man does so refrain, then salvation has not become a full reality in this particular person. Christ's work in such a case is certainly complete and capable of redeeming. But God's part in the individual's salvation is cut off if the person says "no." "The Blood of your Lord has been given for you if you wish it; if you do not wish it, it is not given for you. . . . For him who consents, the Blood of Christ means salvation; for him who does not consent, it means condemnation."[8]

If man does consent, however, and if he concludes the covenant toward which grace has supernaturally urged and disposed him; if man by moral decision takes unto himself the integral, completed, redemptive work of Christ and its fruits, he does something which immediately brings about salvation within him in the fullest sense. Here let us introduce an hypothesis: Let us suppose a person existed whose consent made possible the receiving of Christ's work and its fruit both for himself and for the entire Church. If such were the case, the grace-inspired affirmation would be a co-redemptive contribution, not to Christ's mediation, but certainly such that its effects might be realized in the Church. It is essential, if salvation is to take place, that the Mediator comes to men only if he has been accepted by them.

In this sense it is not wrong to say that man co-operates in his own salvation; that he is a "co-redeemer" of his own salvation. But seen in its entirety it is the Church who is "co-redeemer." It is she who in her totality receives the fullness of redemptive graces and imparts them to those who have been incorporated in her. Mary, the Type of the Church, standing on its pinnacle representing it, pronounces the *fiat* of receptivity and willingness. Thus we can and should truly call her the co-redeemer. But the expression must be understood properly. In the following section more will be said about the correct way of looking at it.

Some Misconceptions

We have seen that a person who at least says "yes" to his own salvation and (to use the words of the theology of grace) "disposes himself," can, to an extent, be correctly called a co-redeemer. This terminology, however, is not commonly used. Man's role during the process of his redemption is too receptive for this active expression to be used freely.

The expression "co-redeemer" has been applied [more] to Mary, although the manner of her actual salvation is essentially like that of other human beings. Pope Benedict XV in his Encyclical *Inter Sodalicias* (1918) writes that one "may truly declare that Mary has redeemed the human race together with Christ."[9] Scheeben "despite a great deal of research could not find this expression anywhere prior to the sixteenth century." He admits, however, that the concept is of some value but does not like to see it used "in a certain sense" without definite limitations, since it tends to place Mary too close to Christ.[10] Actually, the expression "co-redeemer" is so well known and implies so many meanings that it cannot easily be condemned as false. Yet it does not underline Mary's position within the plan of salvation unequivocally. To be able to judge to what extent the title is or is not justified, we will first have to work out carefully the nature of the position that Mary holds in the economy of salvation. We must examine all theological opinions, which to date have been in sharp opposition. Then we will see that both extremes of thought are inadequate. Finally, from Mary's position as Archetype of the Church, we will try to cast some light on her co-redeeming work.

The co-redemption problem has been studied within a theological framework where terminology has perhaps become too rigid. Theologians try to decide whether Mary co-operated with the work of Redemption as a *redemptio objectiva* or only as a *redemptio subjectiva. Redemptio objectiva* means the work of Christ the Redeemer alone; *redemptio subjectiva* means the giving of the fruits of salvation to men when the "proper disposition" (under the influence of grace) makes possible the reception, as well as the increase, of sanctifying grace. The means and vessels instituted by Christ for this process are the sacraments. A. Deneffe, S.J., formulates this briefly in the thesis which he added to the third volume of the *Compendium Theologiae Dogmaticae* by Chr. Pesch, S.J. He says: "*Redemptio objectiva* should be understood as Christ's own work, His Passion and Death, His Sacrifice of the Cross through which He made a reparation to God for man's sins and merited grace for all. *Redemptio subjectiva* is the giving of the fruits of *redemptio objectiva* to individuals."[11] Continuing, he says his thesis on Mary's co-redemption "is to be understood in the light of direct co-operation with objective redemption." Thus, he places Mary beside Christ as a kind of co-principle. She is of course subject to Him but nonetheless she co-operates with His salvation, reparation and redemption. Christ's work is to a certain degree co-constituted through Mary's co-operation or, at any rate, Deneffe's quotation clearly expresses this idea. Not all representatives of this thesis, however, express themselves so unmistakably. Among other writers there is a certain vagueness which envelops this point. Some modify the concept of Mary's primordial co-redemption by stressing her subordination to Christ and underlining the fact that "Christ, the only natural mediator, first had to merit through His bloody Sacrifice all possibility and power of intercession for His mother."[12] Others bring out the correct concept of receptive causality, but then throw a garish spotlight upon Mary's co-causality, her standing beside Christ. This attitude can be seen in Scheuth's very admirable work which, except for this point, expresses correct attitudes.[13]

At any rate we must reject any concept of co-redemption in which Mary is interpreted as really co-meriting grace within Christ's work. Many interpreters definitely do mean just that, for example Koester,[14] Bittremieux,[15] and others. We must reject the idea completely. By it Mary would be the co-worker of her own salvation and she would have to have co-merited to be able to merit at all. A general law would be established saying in effect that Christ's work of Redemption cannot take place without Mary's co-operation. We must remember that Mary herself has been redeemed; and whatever she contributes to salvation is a result of the grace of salvation given her dur-

ing the process of Redemption. Grace is therefore pre-
ceded by Christ's completed work. We may wish to make
Mary an exception to this common law, but it is difficult,
because Mary has been saved by the same Redemption as
have all other human beings. H. Seiler, S.J., writes: "If
Mary co-redeemed man objectively, then we must demonstrate that another sort of objective salvation was established for her alone. We must hold that God redeemed
Mary upon the basis of Christ's self-surrender and that He
redeemed all others on the basis of His self-surrender
through Mary."[16] It is impossible to accept this theory, of
course, nor is such a thesis at all necessary. Lennerz sharply
observes that "one would have to declare that Mary was
not redeemed through the same kind of objective redemption as the rest of mankind. For Mary would not be able to
co-operate if it were not a fact that she was in a state of
grace. But she received this grace through the merit of
Christ, the Redeemer of mankind. One would therefore
have to say that Mary was redeemed through Christ's work
alone; mankind, however, through the work of Christ and
Mary. One would also have to concede that though Mary
bore the *debitum* of original sin in her human nature inherited from Adam—but not imputed to her person—she
was redeemed not in her nature (as in the Redemption of
all other mortals) but by specific redemptive work that applied to her person alone."[17] Smith points out: "When we
are considering Redemption objectively—that is, as meaning the offering of the expiatory and meritorious sacrifice
by which grace again became available for mankind, Our
Lady included—there is room for only a logical distinction

between her redemption and that of anyone else. One and the same price was paid for all."[18]

The mistake (of distinguishing between Mary's redemption and our own) cannot be avoided by pointing out her pre-redemption which would have enabled her to co-operate with Christ's objective salvation. Feckes seems to hold this opinion. He says: "The plan of salvation positively demands the human *fiat* as a first point of contact between the world of God and the world of man; this *fiat*, however, can be made only by the one person to whom this point of contact was made known. Even Mary could accomplish nothing if she were not empowered through her pre-redemption."[19] Here temporal priority—not at issue in our treatment—is confused with causal priority. Even though Mary was pre-redeemed in the temporal sense before the *Logos* entered this world (*propter praevisa merita Christi*, as the Church says), the fact remains that she first had to receive the fruits of the Redemption before being able to fulfill her co-operative role, and Christ's Redemption, with all its satisfactory and meritorious forces, must have been foreseen by God as complete. From this [causal] point of view, God indeed preserved Mary from original sin and pre-redeemed her.

It is impossible, furthermore, to see how the pre-redemptive theory can be reconciled with Holy Scripture. There we find the blunt words that there is only one Mediator between God and man.[20] The question is not of one main Mediator but, simply, *one*. Some proponents of the erroneous co-redemption say: "This should not be understood to mean that Christ could not have redeemed us all alone."[21] This is hardly a pertinent qualification of the doctrine, for Christ was not only able to redeem us Himself, but He actually did redeem us, quite alone. The principle of Redemption is Christ Himself alone; the work of Salvation is His work and His only. The Council of Florence stated in its *Decretum pro Jacobitis* that "Christ alone, who was conceived without sin, was born and died, has through His death killed the enemy of mankind, thereby destroying our sins (*solus una morte prostravit*)."[22] Ambrose answers a hypothetical question that Mary asks of herself: Was there perhaps something that could be added to Christ's public ministry by her own death? The Saint answers: "The suffering of Christ demands no help. The Lord prophesied long ago, 'I looked around and there was no one to help me.' "[23]

Thus, we must not misinterpret Mary's role as the Bride of Christ and as the Second Eve by conceiving her to be a second principle of saving grace which, though subordinate to Christ's, co-operates and co-merits as such. This is true quite apart from the fact that original sin also had only one principle, Adam; Eve, formally speaking, is not a co-principle of original sin. It was Adam alone who transmitted original sin to mankind. There are today and have been many unsolved contradictions in the theory we have sketched above. The interpreters—some of whom we have cited—have labored with difficulties stemming from Scripture, tradition, and ecclesiastical teachings. Nevertheless we must reject the theory which is of no importance in establishing the true "co-redemption" of the Mother of God.

Does this mean that we have to reject any kind of co-redeeming functions the way Goossens,[24] Lennerz,[25] and, at times Bartmann,[26] seem to? Note clearly our words "seem to." Lack of clarity, combined with a too rigorous, unqualified ordering of concepts in these authors, makes it difficult to say that they actually deny any direct co-operation of Mary with salvation. Lennerz admits only a physical and indirect kind of co-operation in the fact that Mary pronounced her *fiat* for the Incarnation.[27] Bartmann attempts to show that Mary's genuine veneration among Catholics is justified because it is based on her relation to Christ as His mother. His effort is to clarify the Catholic position against Protestant reluctance. This leads him to error by defect, for he rejects all co-operation of Mary with the Redemption. Yet, on closer examination, he seems to reject only co-operation with the actual work of Christ Himself and not her co-operation as it is upheld by the Church and which is our own position. For example, this conclusion tends to emerge from the following: "We declare conclusively that Mary's demonstration of faith, seen in its entirety, especially under the Cross, was the price of her meriting life eternal and glory. It is an invaluable model for us, a stimulating example. It should be treated, as it was in later theology, as a quasi-merit or participation in the earning of grace. But both these points presuppose Christ as the unifying head, our sole mediator."[28] Goossens, however, is very categorical in his rejection: "Unless the Church should judge otherwise, one may and should deny the thesis of a direct co-operation with objective redemption."[29]

One must agree with the logic of the objections proposed above if they are understood to mean Mary's direct co-operation with Christ the Redeemer's actual salvation. But a denial of this point of view is not the same as a complete denial of any co-operation on the part of Mary with the Redemption. Such a denial would stand in opposition to both tradition and ecclesiastical *magisterium* (teaching) to the extent that the Church has spoken on the subject up to now. Tradition has stressed the juxtaposition of Mary, the Second Eve, with Eve herself, through whom death came upon the world. This tradition is so uninterrupted and so unanimous that it would be rash to reject it out of hand. The Eve-Mary parallel was intended to suggest some kind of co-operation with the Redemption of the world. As early as Irenaeus, we find explicit testimony, as when he referred to Mary specifically as *"cooperans dispositioni."*[30] To prevent the danger of underestimating this expression, he calls Mary simply the cause of salvation.[31] There is, in fact, no concept applied to Mary and her position in salvation that appears more often than that of the Second Eve. It is unnecessary to quote any more traditional passages on this matter, because the idea is found in the Mariology of all times. When in the course of time other clarifying and specific ideas were introduced, the idea of the Second Eve was never overshadowed.

The Popes of modern times have also taken unto themselves the idea of Mary's co-operation with the Redemption. Leo XIII is especially penetrating on this point when he calls Mary "the worthy co-operator (*administra*) in the accomplishment of the mysteries of salvation."[32] Just as in the teachings of the Fathers on the Second Eve, the Papal documents deal clearly with direct co-operation with the Redemption, not just the imparting of its fruits to individuals. Therefore, a complete denial of Mary's co-operation (except for the imparting of fruits) would not do justice to these papal texts. Scheeben is quite correct when he says: "There is an ancient ecclesiastical concept, attested to a thousand times, or rather, an explicitly documented dogma resulting from the way the Protogospel was taught in the Vulgate (*ipsa conteret caput tuum*), that states that the effects of Christ's Redemption should be attributed in a very real sense to His Mother, as a principle."[33]

Of course, both the papal and traditional texts need not mean and should not mean an immediate co-operation with the so-called objective Redemption, if this is understood according to Lennerz, Deneffe, and others as Christ's work only. Then it would seem that Christ did not perform His work alone after all. Both extreme views are based on a narrow concept of the essence of the Church. She is thought of as merely a collection of many redeemed individuals and this concept does not do her justice. Such a view offers only an either-or chioce between co-operation with the work of the Redeemer on the one hand and the application of its fruit to individuals on the other. Accordingly, any denial of direct co-operation with *redemptio objectiva* would by its nature admit only the imparting of the fruits to individuals. On the other hand, if more than an imparting to individuals were meant, the conclusion would follow that direct co-operation is involved. The fact remains that the Church is not clearly understood as the living entity that serves as the link between the work of Christ and man's participation in it. That is precisely where Mary stands; she is the Type of the truly co-redeeming Church which gives salvation.

True Co-Redemption

If God's eternal plan were for Mary to be the Archetype, she must above all typify the Church in the essential functions given to the Church in Christ's plan for salvation. From this vantage point, discussion of Mary's participation should receive some elucidation, for we have seen that it has bogged down and has been treated in a far too systematized and rigid manner. Certainly, it would not be fitting that Mary the Archetype should have co-operated with Redemption in any other way than does the Church herself.

The difficulty in Mary's participation arises more from the question of her co-operation and mediation of graces than from the inner core of the archetypal mystery. We will see that everything falls with meaningful, indeed necessary, logic into the entire scheme of salvation. But we will not reach this clarity until Mary's co-operation has been firmly grasped in the ecclesiological sense. In other words, her co-operation was influenced by the graces flowing from the completed work of salvation; she took them unto herself in her subjective, moral re-enactment of what Christ wrought. Simultaneously, she received the fruit of His work. There is cloudiness in the terminology and expositions of the authors who prefer the theory of Mary's direct co-operation with *redemptio subjectiva,* and this lack of clarity dominates their treatment of the entire problem of co-redemption and co-operation. Despite this, however, it must be admitted that these rather extreme views can be understood in a correct sense, until we suddenly run head on into a spate of words that casts the entire issue into an untenable position. Let us take an example. Bittremieux draws a simple parallel between Mary's mediation and that of Christ. This is impossible. It bears an inner contradiction and is opposed to Revelation: "Christ is the main Mediator, Mary is a secondary Mediator; thus, Mary's mediatorship must be stressed as parallel to Christ's but none the less subordinate to His."[34] The fact that Bittremieux and others stress this "subordinated" role makes the whole matter look rather suspicious. The correct view of Mary's function as mediator leaves her in her most natural and close relationship to Christ. This relationship is the same as that of the *Ecclesia* and there need be no emphasis on subordination, for Christ's role is in no way in danger.

The essence of the Church's task within God's plan casts light on Mary's role within salvation. The Church's innermost essence—determining and causing everything else—should be the fact that she is the community of men redeemed in Christ. To the extent that man has participated in Christ's Redemption, he has become the Church. Redemption in Christ embraces the material as well as the spiritual side; both the visible organization and the interior divine life belong fully and essentially to the Church. Tradition has always held that the Church is the community of men redeemed in Christ and, accordingly, the Church is considered to have been in existence prior to Christ's historical life. After all, there are human beings redeemed in Christ before His era. The idea of the Mystical Body of Christ (as seen in the contemporary interest in St. Paul and in Pius XII's Encyclical *Mystici Corporis*) best describes the Church's essence. The same point is stressed: The Church is the community of men in Christ who have grown together in a mystical-realistic and supernatural way. The Church is the union of men who have been joined to the Mystical Christ for and through the reception of the fruits of salvation. Note this exceptional statement: "Through the Church every man performs a work of collaboration with Christ in dispensing the graces of Redemption, thus acting as 'co-redeemer.' "[35]

The fact that the Church is a community of the redeemed, however, does not mean that she exists because redeemed men exist. She is not a gathering of a number of redeemed individuals. Quite the contrary. Men are redeemed because and to the extent that they have a place within her as a living entity. Ecclesiastical tradition brings vividly to mind the idea that the Church represents the one total Christ in whose Redemption individual man has a part by being incorporated into that very entity. Thus, in this case, totality really precedes the individual parts.

Here we have the inner reason why the sacramental nature of marriage is founded on the bond between Christ and His Church. Salvation is marital. God wants to save man. He does not want to overpower his will but rather summon him to make his own decision. Humanity is to receive the *Logos* who comes to establish the covenant. It then has to take on the work that the *Logos* is performing in its midst. Insofar as man gives his *fiat*, he becomes the Church, the Bride of the *Logos* and the God-man. Augustine recognized that a real marriage bond was consummated between the divinity of Christ and the human nature of Mary. This bond offers all mankind to God's *Logos* in salvation, thus enabling Him to be received by humanity. "In the bridal chamber, that is in the womb of the Virgin, divine Nature united itself to human nature when the Word became flesh for us."[36]

Because the *Logos* entered into humanity, the Church has not ceased to confront Him with her own kind of independent decision. The work performed by the God-man within humanity (in His function of sacrificial priest before the Father), is His work. It would remain exclusively His work even if mankind (prompted by grace but still free in decision) did not accept it. The grace which bears humanity up does not impair its own decision to take Christ's sacrifice upon itself as its own. This relation is like the bride's act of love for the bridegroom. This is the ultimate redeeming factor. Indeed, Christ's sacrifice rises up to the Father from the midst of mankind to which He belongs. For his sacrifice to become man's it must be assumed subjectively by man.

The essential task of the Church, therefore, is to assume Christ's work as His Bride and thereby to participate in its fruits. Accordingly the Church is co-redemptive in the truest sense. If she were not, Christ's work—though certainly capable of saving—would not effectively save anyone. The Church co-operates with Redemption—but not in a productive way, for Christ alone does this. The Church's co-operation is receptive—which does not imply passivity alone: a point that should never be forgotten. This is the inner substance of the covenant. Revelation shows this quite clearly when it calls the Church the Bride of Christ. The fact that the characteristics of the Church as the Bride of Christ and as Christ's Mystical Body[37] are so closely united shows that humanity must exercise its self-determination and grace-inspired, free co-operation

in Redemption. This is true despite Christ's sole produc-
tivity by which He accomplishes the mystical-physical,
organic union of Himself and humanity within the Church.
Humanity's exercise of choice in co-operation is so essential that Christ's redeeming activity and His Church's co-
redeeming activity seem like an interchange of effectiveness.

By co-operating with the Redemption in taking Christ's
work and fruits upon itself humanity becomes the Church
filled with Christ's *pleroma*. It stands before Him as one
great wholeness. Since the Church lives within a world
extended in time and space, Christ's work must be taken up
in time and space. His sacrifice is one only. "Jesus having
offered one sacrifice for sins"[38] "by virtue of His own
blood, entered once and for all into the Holy of Holies,
having obtained eternal redemption."[39] This one sacrifice
must unfold within a Church growing in time and space
into multiple single acts from the one sacramental event.
The sacraments raise Christ's work from its historical and
temporal setting to a supra-temporal level of mystery. At
the same time they extend the work within the space-time
confines of our own earthly existence. Christ's one Church
—despite the multiplicity of its outward appearance—is the
same as it was nineteen hundred years ago, as it is today,
and as it will be at the end of time. The Church is the
Bride of Christ who lives because of the *fiat* she pronounces
to her Bridegroom's work; receiving His fruits she is joined
to Him in the mystical-physical oneness of His Mystical
Body.

The oneness of the Church, her quasi-personality,
through which she performs her saving function of re-

demptive co-operation, is seen represented and realized in
Mary. The Church, the Bride of Christ, must confront
Him as a personal figure and seize hold of the work fully
accomplished by Him alone. Here Mary's function enters.
She gives her consent to the approaching *Logos* because,
redeemed and endowed with His grace, she is able to do so.
Because she gives her affirmation for the coming of the
Logos and for Christ's Sacrifice, she has taken on the work
of Christ and made its fruits of grace her own. These
gifts are ours "through Christ's death alone."[40] But Mary's
co-operation with her own redemption is performed by
her for herself, and through her as representative of the
humanity which is to become the Church—"in the place
of the entire human race."[41] Mary, that is to say the
Church, has become "disposed" for the reception of the
Arch-sacrament, the Incarnate God and His sacrifice on
the Cross. Because of this receptivity, or rather through
it, "the fullness of all blessings has been deposited in her;"[42]
that is to say, the *pleroma* that fills the Church. This can
be the only meaning Pius X had in mind when he says that
Mary merited "*de congruo*" what Christ merited "*de condigno*."[43] The pertinent pronouncements of the more recent Popes (Leo XIII, Pius X, Benedict XV and Pius XI)
can be interpreted only according to the ecclesiological
concept of co-redemption as we have demonstrated it.
They cannot be understood according to the pattern of
co-operation with either objective or subjective redemption, if these concepts are understood in the way we have
outlined them. This can be seen clearly in the expositions
and interpretations of H. Seiler, S.J., although he tries
to find direct co-operation with objective redemption in

the limited sense, and thinks he has his proof in Benedict XV and Pius XI.[44] But he is in error. The papal pronouncements can be interpreted clearly and with no difficulty from the ecclesiological point of view.

Thus, Mary co-operated with the Church's Redemption by her receptive causality. In the realization of Redemption, this causality is a true one. It is a very real and essential causality, just as man's receptive, actively disposing co-operation is regarding his own blessedness. Seiler says that "only insofar as Mary has co-offered Christ's Sacrifice on the Cross so that she co-operated—at the very least—with His reparation objectively and co-merited all graces objectively, is she a co-redeemer in the true sense of the word."[45] If this were true we would have to reject any real co-redemption on Mary's part. But the presumption is inaccurate, certainly if active co-redemption is understood to mean that Mary, acting as co-principle beside Christ, would then stand confronting a recipient Church. This is not demanded of her because the Church also is co-redeemer in a real and true sense, although not in the way Seiler's thought would have it.

Our exposition has been in accord with tradition's constant view of Mary's function: receiving and giving the Life that conquered Eve's deed. The Fathers hold Mary to be the cause of salvation because of her receptivity—based on her active belief—to the coming of the *Logos* and the accomplishment of His work. In the words of Irenaeus, Mary becomes the *Advocata Evae*, the solicitor of mankind awaiting Redemption, a mankind which must open itself for the work of the Redemption and which actually did so in Mary. Peter Chrysologus formulated

Mary's position when he spoke of her as the pinnacle of humanity enabling it to become the Church by her *fiat*, her reception of the Redeemer and His work and its fruits, and by passing these on into the Church prefigured by her. He declares briefly: "The Virgin received salvation in order to pass it on through the centuries."[46] The Scholastic theologians also wanted to stress this idea of receptive co-operation typical of the Church. When commenting on the *Ave Maria*, St. Thomas contrasts Mary's co-operation and plenitude of grace to the first Eve's co-operation with sinfulness. Eve searched for the fruit but did not find what she was looking for. Mary found it through her co-operation with Redemption. What Mary found made her full of grace, *"ad refusionem ad omnes homines."*

Eve sought the fruit but in this fruit she did not find what she was looking for at all. But the Blessed Virgin found in her fruit what Eve had been seeking. [This is a clear indication that Mary was co-operating receptively for mankind who was going to be saved.] Eve sought three things from her fruit. First, she wanted what the Devil had falsely promised her—that they should become like gods, knowing good and evil. . . . In eating her fruit, Eve did not become like God but unlike Him. As a result of her sin, she abandoned God and her salvation, and was driven from Paradise. But the Blessed Virgin and all Christians found salvation in the fruit of her body, for through Christ we are united to God and likened to Him . . . . Second, Eve sought delight in her fruit because it was good to eat. This satisfaction she did not find, for she suddenly found herself naked and sensed pain. But in the fruit of the Virgin, we find sweetness and salvation. Third, Eve's fruit was beautiful to look at. But even more beautiful is the Fruit of the Virgin which angels long to contemplate. Eve did not find what she wanted in her fruit; a sinner does not find what he wants in his sinfulness. This is why we seek our fulfillment in the Fruit of the Virgin. And this Fruit is blessed by God for He has filled it with all graces and came down to us and adored God.[47]

This concept of Mary's co-operation with Redemption, placing her on the peak of humanity, in no way diminishes the position of Christ as Head of the Church. Mary's co-operation is a receptive, active appropriation of Christ's work under the influence of grace meant for her and for the whole Church. And the Church becomes the Body of Christ only insofar as she confronts Him in a personal, bridal attitude. This entire structure is supported by Scheeben, even though in other presentations he is sometimes lacking in necessary clarity of expression. "Mary's co-operation is apparently not needed for the constitution or completion of the inner potency of the Redemption. Rather, it is needed for the total completion of the beauty and loveliness of the work of the Redemption. This is particularly so for the perfecting of the organic connection with humanity awaiting Redemption, and on that connection the whole perfection of its application and applicability depends."[48]

If—in spite of the inherent inadequacies of the terms— what we have developed here were to be ordered according to the traditional terminology of *redemptio objectiva* and *redemptio subjectiva*, we would say the following: Mary co-operated directly, not with *redemptio objectiva*, if by this term we mean the work of Christ alone; and not with *redemptio subjectiva*, as long as this term is taken to mean only the application of the fruits of redemption to individual men. Rather, Mary co-operated with her own *redemptio objectiva*, which redemption, however, *simultaneously signifies* the reception of the fruits of salvation for the entire Church and which is therefore objective with regard to the individual.

If we want to formulate this into a thesis we can say: Mary is the Type of the Church which imparts salvation, insofar as by assuming the work of Christ she receives the fruits of that work both for herself and for the whole Church.

NOTES

1. Feckes, C., *Das Mysterium der heiligen Kirche* (Paderborn, 1935), p. 268.
2. *Die Magd des Herrn. Theologische Versuche und Ueberlegungen* (Limburg, 1947), p. 7.
3. De la Taille, S.J., M., *Mysterium fidei* (Paris, 1924), p. 648. Eng. trans., *Mystery of Faith* (New York, Sheed and Ward, 1930).
4. Gal. 4,6.
5. Ezek. 16.
6. Matt. 26,28.
7. Koester, H.M., *Die Magd des Herrn*, p. 77.
8. St. Augustine, *Sermo* 344, n. 4. – ML 39, 1515.
9. *A. A. S.* (1918), 182.
10. *Dogmatik* III, n. 1775.
11. Editio VI (Freiburg, 1940), p. 305.

12. Pohle-Gierens, *Lehrbuch der Dogmatik* (Paderborn, 1936), II, p. 308.

13. *Mediatrix. Eine mariologische Frage* (Innsbruck, 1925).

14. Article "Maria" in *Lexikon fuer Theologie und Kirche* (Freiburg).

15. *De mediatione universali B.M.V. quoad gratias* (Brugis, 1926).

16. *Corredemptrix. Theologische Studie zur Lehre der letzten Paepste ueber die Miterloeserschaft Mariens* (Rome, 1939), p. 32.

17. "De redemptione et cooperatione in opere redemptionis," in: *Gregorianum*, 22 (1941), p. 322.

18. Smith, G.D., *Mary's Part in Our Redemption* (New York, Kenedy, 1938), and translated by B. Erasmi, *Die Stellung Mariens im Erloesungswerk Christi* (Paderborn, 1947), p. 135.

19. "Das Fundamentalprinzip der Mariologie," in: *Scientia sacra*, Festscrift fuer Kardinal Schulte (Koeln-Duesseldorf, 1935), p. 268.

20. 1 Tim. 2,5.

21. Preising, R., *Erfuellung in Christus. Die Kirche als mystischer Herrenleib* (Paderborn, 1947), p. 72.

22. Denzinger 711.

23. *De institutione virginis*, cap. VII. – Ml 16, 333 B.

24. *De cooperatione immediata Matris redemptoris ad redemptionem objectivam* (Paris, 1939).

25. *De Beata Virgine. Ad usum auditorum* (Rome, 1935). "De redemptione et cooperatione in opere redemptionis" in: *Gregorianum*, 22 (1941).

26. *Christus ein Gegner des Marienkults?* (Freiburg, 1909).

27. "De redemptione et cooperatione in opere redemptionis," p. 313.

28. *Christus ein Gegner des Marienkults?*, p. 158.

29. *De cooperatione immediata Matris redemptoris ad redemptionem objectivam*, p. 128.

30. *Adversus haereses* III. 21.7. – MG 7, 953 B.

31. *Ibid.* III, 22,4. – MG 7, 959 A.

32. "Adjutricem populi," *ASS* 28 (1895–96), p. 130.

33. *Dogmatik* III, n. 1771.

34. *De mediatione universali B.M.V. quoad gratias*, p. 14.

35. Pius XII, *Mystici corporis*, n. 12.

36. Augustine, *Sermo* 193, n. 3. – ML 38, 1019.

37. Eph. 5,25–33.

38. Hebr. 10,12.

39. Hebr. 9,12.

40. Pius X, *Ad diem illum, ASS* 36 (1903–04), p. 453.

41. Thomas of Aquinas, *S. th.* III, q. 30, a. 1.

42. Leo XIII, *Supremi apostolatus. ASS* 16 (1883), p. 118.

43. *Ad diem illum*, p. 452.

44. *Corredemptrix. Theologische Studie zur Lehre der letzten Paepste ueber die Miterloeserschaft Mariens* (Rome, 1939), pp. 51ff.

45. *Op. cit.*, p. 26.

46. *Sermo* 143. – ML 52, 583 C.

47. *In salutationem angelicam.*

48. *Dogmatik* III, n. 1783.

CHAPTER 4

Mediator

The fact that man receives no grace without Mary's co-operation may present no problem whatever to the average member of the Church. But the opposite is true of a man who tries to probe more deeply into his faith. He is frequently heard to ask: Why should the relationship between God and man be made complicated? Why should there be this difficulty caused by the addition of an unnecessary middle person? Should we not assume that the God of primordial simplicity would want simplicity to rule the life He shares with man? Doesn't it seem that this addition of a mediator is the sign of a piety that exchanges multiplicity and complications for rich vitality? Doesn't it seem that a piety which continues to introduce new objects of veneration is alien to both the early Christian tradition of the Church and to the essential meaning of Christendom itself?

This objection may sound convincing at first and cast some doubt upon Mary's almost obvious position as Mediator of Graces. Actually, however, the objection is based on a mistaken judgment of Mary's mediation. We cannot separate Mary's function as Mediator from the function of the Church as Mediator. Here above all we see Mary herself as Type of the Church. If a person's thinking is dominated by

the Protestant concept of the Church as a gathering of individual sanctified men, it will be difficult to see that the
Church has the power to impart salvation and that she lies
as an intermediary between the individual life of grace and
its divine Source. But according to our recently re-acquired
understanding of the Church's essence, it is not at all difficult to see the Church as Mediator of salvation. From this
point of view also, Mary's position as the Mediator of all
graces—stemming particularly from her role as Archetype
of the Church—should not offer any difficulties either to
the mind or to any resulting religious observance. In the
next section, our first task will be to examine the manner in
which the Church provides salvation. This must be more a
study of the Church as the Lord's Mystical Body, necessarily giving life to the incorporated individual parts, rather
than a consideration of her as an institution of salvation.
The correct view of the Church's function in giving salvation will also throw light on Mary's mediatorship of salvation. The Protestant Hase was right when he said: "It is in
Mary that the Catholics defend their concept of the
Church's mediation of graces."[1]

The Church Imparts Salvation

The historical mission of nominalism in re-establishing the
right of the individual and the personality should certainly
not be misunderstood. The development of this system of
thought, however, caused a gradual loss of the Church's
awareness of her own inner essence. It is easier to understand why the Reformation theologians, influenced by nom-

inalism, broke away from the Church, once one realizes how strong the influence of this theology was. These theologians saw the Church simply as an assembly of the redeemed. And their concept of "assembly" was secondary. In this view, the Church is nothing more than a gathering of people who happen to be holy—not a living organism into which man must first be incorporated in order to become holy.

Catholic theology of that era followed a similar trend of thought and was itself strongly influenced by nominalism. The dispute with Protestantism, therefore, became centered on the Protestant refusal to recognize the Church as a visible organization, even though this reasoning on the part of Catholic theology was hardly representative of the innermost essence of the Church. The apologetics of the four centuries after the Reformation hardly stressed the fact that the Church is Our Lord's Mystical Body to whom all must be united if they are to participate in salvation. Rather, the emphasis of the apologists was on man's physical surroundings and the whole cosmos. They reasoned that because these too have a part in salvation,[2] Christ's Church must include everything visible and perceptible. She must also have a visible unity. Thus apologetics opposed to the spiritualistic denial of the visible element in the Church differed very little from that of the antagonists, who considered the Church to be the gathering of individual, redeemed men. The visible organization of the Church had to be proven as being established by Christ. Then its interior life had to be explained on the basis of man's dependence on the visibility of supernatural salvation, the necessity of a unified guidance, etc. Even the visible community of the Church is explained from the standpoint of the individual and the individual's blessedness is given priority, while in the realm of asceticism man's sanctification is a matter between God and man alone. While this latter point cannot be called totally incorrect, it is open to danger and misunderstanding. Finally, the individualistic concept of the Church finds its sharpest expression in the more or less deliberately formulated view that the Church is endowed only with the juridical and pastoral duties of the guidance of souls, the care of the flock, and the pronouncement of truth.

It did not occur to the apologists and theologians of this individualistic era that the only real way to oppose a correspondingly false and individualistic idea of the Church was to return to the true concept of the Church's essence, the supernatural organism of Christ's Mystical Body. Questions on the reason of the Church's existence were advanced and answered in a way that made her look too much like an institution. Or else, she appeared as a third entity between two polarities—a ready instrument used by God to endow man with something, or, even more mistakenly, as something to be used by man to gain salvation. Pilgram, a lay theologian of the past century, was ahead of his time. In his long expositions he fought the concept of the Church as an institution of salvation.[3] But even today the dogmatic and theological understanding of the Church's essence is an area that waits for a necessary profound revision. The faithful are still a long way from seeing themselves as the Church. The Church, in turn, seems to face them like a court of authority where the Word of God is pronounced and the sacraments are given out. The faithful do not know themselves as members of the

Church and as redeemed by her. Nor do they realize that they take part in the sacramental, grace-filled life of Christ's Mystical Body.

This individualistic concept of the Church cannot penetrate into Mary's real position as Mediator. But the Church's self-knowledge, which at this moment is formulating a more definite and clearer expression of her very essence, justifies hope for Mariological insight. It is astonishing to compare Pius XII's Encyclical *Mystici Corporis* and the many apologetic tracts on the Church. However, we will have to try once more to see the unity of all humanity realistically. This is the way it is presented by Revelation, with Adam the head of mankind and with Christ the new Head who recapitulates all human history. We will have to try to make that divine vision of humanity our own by contemplating the supernatural unity of the world of Redemption. To be sure, the human personality, the individual standpoint limited by its juxtaposition to another ego, remains inviolable. But just as inviolable is the truth that the human ego receives its actual graces only when it is linked to the Church's redeeming wholeness in mystical-physical and organic unity. Man must not first be reborn and thereby become a member of the Church. Rather, the reverse is true. Because and insofar as man is a member of the Church, he receives divine life. Irenaeus says of those participating in the Redemption: "They are rightly begotten because they were converted to God's Church and thus Christ is formed in them."[4]

The Encyclical *Mystici Corporis* refuses to call the Church's Mystical Body a physical body. But this certainly does not refute the fact that the Church is a real organism, a true entity formed by the members who are accepted within it before they became morally active. The physical concept is refuted because in such a union "the principle of unity unites the parts so that each lacks its own individual substance. In the Mystical Body, on the contrary, the mutual union—though intrinsic—links the members by a bond leaving each his own personality intact."[5] But the Church does not define her union as a moral one only; this point is just as sharply denied. The strongly individualistic concept of the Church in the centuries following the Reformation is certainly not the complete truth. "The word 'mystical' in its correct meaning leads us to understand that the Church is not made up of merely moral and juridical elements and principles."[6] In a moral body the principal union is nothing more than the common end and the common co-operation of all under authority for the attainment of that end. In the Mystical Body, on the other hand, this collaboration is supplemented by a distinct internal principal which exists effectively in the whole and in each of its parts. Its excellence is such that of itself it is vastly superior to whatever bonds of union may be found in a physical or moral body. . . . The Angelic Doctor says, "The Spirit of God, numerically one and the same, fills and unifies the entire Church."[7] Thus we can say unequivocally that the whole organism and the individual parts are filled by this one Principle. Thus it is at once clear that the totality of the Church is much more than the result of individual members gathered together. The Church as a whole has first place in the process of salvation. The Church exists as a whole, and individual man has a part in the life of salvation because he is rooted in that whole.

Thus, the commonly employed concept of mediatorship is not incorrect, but it can only be applied to the Church in an analogous sense. The Church, Christ's Body, is a mediator of all those graces destined for individuals whom Christ possesses as Head of the human race. The Church receives human beings into her vitally supernatural life-community filled with Christ's *pleroma* and she imparts her life, the life of Christ, to them as a vine to its branches. The simple statement that an intermediary cannot be identified with one of the two extreme points which are being connected is a misunderstanding. Equally incorrect would be an unqualified insistence on the opposite point of view. Those to whom mediation is extended can be members of the one whole which does the mediating. This is what happens in the Church.

If we look upon the Redemption as the covenant concluded between God and man, the Church appears before her divine-human Partner as a entity. She is His Bride. Every single community within the Church participates in this bridal character in relation to Christ. St. Paul expresses it very clearly to the Corinthians: "I betrothed you to one spouse that I might present you as a chaste virgin to Christ."[8] The same statement can be applied to every member of the Church, though it may be better to call the member a child of the Church because, seen as a whole, she is a mother (or mediator).

Even the subhuman, corporeal world participates in redemption within the Church. "Created nature has been condemned to frustration; not for some deliberate fault of its own, but through him who so condemned it."[9] Man used created nature for his rebellion against God. This same created nature will have a part in redemption if its hope finds fulfillment in "the revelation of the children of God." Cosmic creation is also included in the Church and thus has a part in salvation which is only imparted in and through the Church. According to her innermost essence the Church is a visible organization, a corporeal entity, and thus she has to be because the whole cosmos is drawn into the salvation of which she is the bearer.

Thus, the Church is the mediator of all graces of the Redemption. But the Church does not act like a third authority between two poles, or as a messenger going from one to another without becoming involved herself. The Church is mediator of all graces because she bears the fullness of these graces within herself, and individual man participates in these graces as a member of the Church. The vine as a whole transmits its life pulsations to the branches.

This organic oneness and totality of the Church is not only morally but mystically real. Yet it would remain vague and unreal for us if its oneness did not become visible in a tangible figure. The history of salvation which contains the essential covenant with God has shown us repeatedly that "God moves toward the whole by means of isolated and pre-ordained counterpoints, which, though emerging from Him, remain connected with Him and mark and sustain all things. Examples of what we mean here would be individual personalities or groups of persons, who, because of their mission, their importance as first comers, or the fullness of their being, contain, personify, and present the totality of the larger mystery within themselves. They gather multiplicity into oneness."[10] Mary is the individual personal figure in whom the Church is gathered into oneness. She approaches Christ as His Bride and assumes His work with her *fiat*. In our modern way of thinking, Mary personifies the Church as a symbol. But more than this, she personifies the Church as the primordial cell from which the Church extends in time and space. In her the Church is gathered into a juridically representative oneness. But Mary is also joined into a real mystical oneness because she possesses the plenitude of graces which overflow from her into the Church. This plenitude is Christ's; it is His *pneuma*. Thus there is no question of a Marian-Mystical Body. Rather, it is a Marian-bridal element within the Mystical Body of Christ.

Mary, Mediator of All Graces

On the feast of the Seven Sorrows of Mary, the Church prays: "Through thee, O Virgin Mary, let us draw salvation from the wounds of Christ."[11] Thus the Church affirms in her prayer the expression "to Jesus through Mary." In the minds of the faithful, however, the phrase is interpreted to mean from the direction of men to Christ. This prayer of the Seven Sorrows shows that the direction from Christ to men has equal validity. Some Catholics still refuse to recognize Mary's mediatorship of all graces; theological study is still trying to clarify this expression by establishing its connection to the entire scheme of salvation. Yet Feckes does not hesitate to say that the fact of Mary's mediatorship is "today the common property of all theologians."[12]

This is exactly what Benedict XIV meant when he said that Mary is "like a heavenly stream on whose waves all graces and gifts for us unhappy mortals are borne."[13] Although recent Popes from Leo XIII to Pius XII have continued to develop similar comparisons, nothing new is being proposed. Benedict XIV's "heavenly stream" suggests comparison with Bernard of Clairvaux's "channel" through which Christ's graces flow to His Church. Scholasticism is well acquainted with the idea that Mary possesses the fullness of graces that flow into the Church. The Patristic tradition also does not limit Mary's intermediary function to her free acceptance of faith in the divine Word. The brilliant orator, Cyril of Alexandria, in his speech against Nestorius, expressed the opinion that the interchange between God and man takes place through Mary in both directions. He says, "Through Mary the *Trias* is sanctified, and through her the Cross is honored and venerated in the entire *Oekumene*"; "Through her the fallen creature is taken up to heaven." Even the action of the sacramental graces is not excluded: "Through Mary, Baptism is administered to the faithful"; "through her nations are being converted."[14] Thus, we see Cyril's concept of the twofold action of Mary's mediatorship, that is, from man to God and from God to man. The brilliance of Cyril's rhetoric in no way diminishes the reality of the idea of "everything through Mary."

This more profound understanding of Mary's position and work will clarify our concept of Christ's work and prevent us from paying homage to a human being that is due to Christ alone. We will also be able to come closer to the answer as to why God placed Mary in this proximity to Christ instead of leaving all to the mediatory position of the God-man. The final plea that all depends on the purely positive Will of God, the Founder of Salvation, will be the ultimate answer only when the boundary of the Mystery prevents us from penetrating any further.

Let us begin by investigating the reason behind Mary's mediatorship with the fact that she is the Archetype. Mary as Archetype of the Church is, like the Church, mediator of all graces. We can isolate three ways in which her grace-giving functions are typical of the Church. The three functions, however, belong organically together because actually they are in some way one. First, as co-redeemer (in the sense presented in the last chapter), Mary received the fruits of Christ's salvation and assumed them for herself and the Church. Second, she permits these fruits to flow into the Church for men—this we call her "intercession." Finally, she is a mediator through her typical example, which induces the individual within the Church to face his Redeemer with the basic prayer of acceptance. This means that man must co-operate with his own redemption the way Mary co-operated with the redemption of the entire Church.

Mary's role in Redemption—her task as co-redeemer—has far too often been separated from her universal mediatorship of graces. If, for reasons of method, these two topics have had to be treated separately, they should not be understood as a double reality. The fact that grace moved Mary to assume the work of Christ, the fact that she is thereby the Church's representative, is the principle of her grace-giving function—indeed it is that very function itself. Mary accepted in her own spirit the work of sacrifice which Christ alone performed. Thus, this sacrifice became the sacrifice and satisfaction offered by the Church.

This can be the only meaning of Pius X's statement that "Mary merited for us *de congruo* what Christ merited *de condigno*."[15] Pope Pius explained this mutuality by using the phrase "according to Christ's and Mary's mutual suffering and direction of will." But this phrase must not be understood to mean that Christ and Mary in mutual meriting had both obtained the grace of Redemption, except that Mary merited only in a lesser way. Mary would then be on the same level with Christ, acting as a co-principle of grace. She would then be confronting the Church, which is the recipient of His grace. This has been a source of frequent misunderstanding. As a result Mary's position has not always been completely comprehensible.

Actually, Mary, as Type and pinnacle of the Church, affirmed Christ's work and thereby disposed both herself and the Church within her for the *pleroma* of salvation. A meriting *de congruo* cannot be taken in a narrow sense. Rather, it must be interpreted very analogously, for analogy does not permit placing Mary beside Christ on the level of a common gaining of grace. The so-called meriting *de congruo* is the only kind of positive disposition according to which man, empowered by grace, receives as a human being that which Christ does and obtains. This can be the only meaning Scheeben has in mind when he says: "The term mediator should not be applied to Mary in the sense in which it is applied to other Saints. Rather, it should be applied analogously, as in the case of Christ Himself. This means that Mary should be characterized as the intermediary cause of all the effects of salvation for all men, even for pre-Christian mankind and especially for the First Parents. Accordingly, Mary should be called mediator, not

only because she imparts fruits of salvation but also because she mediates in their creation and procurement as
well."[16] If Mary's subjective, personal co-performance of
Christ's work and her resulting reception of its fruits as
depositum for the entire Church (as Scheeben himself once
said) is understood to mean a mediation in the creation and
procurement of these fruits, the above statement can be
understood correctly.

By virtue of her being the true Type of the Church,
Mary's *redemptio subjectiva* (to use the Scholastic term) is
a fullness of grace for the whole Church. Mary stands as an
official personality, as the Church's representative beneath
the Cross (and not only in a juridical sense, although this
too has a very real basis). Here she receives the plenitude
of redemptive grace for the entire Church. Here she becomes the Mother of mankind, which is growing into the
future Church. She is the essence, the primordial cell, from
which life abounds. "The mystery of Christ's boundless
love for us has also been clearly revealed by the fact that at
His death He entrusted His Mother to the care of His dis-
ciple John when He spoke His last Will: 'Behold thy son.'
It is the uninterrupted belief of the Church that Christ saw
in the young John the whole human race, especially those
men who are united to Him in faith."[17]

This interpretation of Mary's mediation is held by the
eminent theologians of Scholasticism. They do not put
much emphasis on her mediation in the sense of her constant
supplication, although this aspect of her intercession, inherent in her position as mediator, is present. The center of
their emphasis is the fact that Mary is the one who became
the recipient of grace because of her receptive co-operation

with the Redemption. Mary is "full of grace" in the triple sense that St. Thomas developed in his *Expositio in Salutationem Angelicam:*

> Mary is called full of grace in a threefold sense: First, with regard to her soul which contains the entire fullness of grace, because grace is given for a double purpose, namely to do good and avoid evil, and the Blessed Virgin possessed perfect grace. . . . Second, Mary was full of the grace that overflows to the body. Saints are endowed with grace for the sanctification of the soul, but the Blessed Virgin was so full of grace that it overflowed into her flesh, enabling it to receive the Son of God. . . . Third, Mary possesses grace that overflows to all men. Every saint has enough grace to sanctify many men. But if he had so much that it could sanctify all men, this indeed would be a miracle. But this is precisely the case with Christ and the Blessed Virgin.

This thought (further developed by Bonaventure and other theologians of the Scholastic period) clearly elucidates the fact that Mary received grace through the receptive manner of her co-operation in the Redemption, in order to let it flow from her into the Church and then become extended in time and place. The Scholastics' concept of mediation was very realistic. Their stress was not only upon the juridical-personal interpretation which has dominated our contemporary nominalistic mentality as the only way of transmitting grace. No, Scholastic opinion states clearly that Mary transmits graces through her personal intervention. But it also sees very realistically that she is the depository for the plenitude of all graces for the Church. Even if a given theology is unable to rise above the juridical concept, the essential nature of Mary's mediation of graces would not be lessened through the fact of her co-redemption. In such a theological construct, Mary's subjective acceptance of Christ's sacrifice would enable her to receive the fruits of salvation for the whole Church. Her personal intercession would have gained her the right to impart graces to the Church and her members within time.

Mary entered into eternity as Type of the Church and with her "creaturely" receptive attitude intact. She remains unchanged. St. Paul says that Christ stands before the Father living on "ever to make intercession on our behalf;"[18] or, to use the idiom of piety, showing His wounds to His Father. Mary stands as the perpetual *Orante* in the eternally changeless attitude of the Church's receptivity before Christ and she receives what the Church needs. When we visualize this attitude we tend to imagine Mary as a pleading mediator. This is because our limited minds have to partition unchangeable eternity into a multiplicity of single events. We soon realize that our image is analogous and anthropocentric and applies to only one side of a complex reality. Mary receives the Church's *pleroma* and lets it flow through the Church, but in this case she is acting as a person, not as a lifeless channel. The image of prayerful intercession is best suited to characterize the one historical acceptance of salvation's *pleroma* which continues to exist in eternity and is acted out simultaneously in the Church during its temporal life in the world. One fact is certainly established through Mary's position as the receptive co-redeemer—"that from the great treasury of all graces merited for us by Our Lord nothing is given to us except through Mary."[19] Our imaginative picture of her constant supplication divided among the pleas of different individuals is but the anthropomorphic representation of one permanent reality whereby she "continuously performs the function of receiving graces for us from God"[20] as the Archetype of the Church.

Seen from the viewpoint of her position as Archetype, Mary's mediation of graces becomes very logical and intelligible. We can agree with Koester who says: "Interpreted and defined in the context of the history of salvation, Mary emerges very clearly as a spontaneous consequence of the order of salvation. This consequence is so natural that any denial of it would seem strange and would have to bear the burden of proof."[21]

Every believer must dispose himself—through his own receptivity—for participation with the grace of Redemption and thus co-operate with his own redemption. Here again an imitation of Mary's attitude is required (for the individual and the Church); consequently her grace-giving function, even in her position as Archetype, is a moral example. This moral efficacy (once given an extremely one-sided emphasis by a heresy connected with Pelagianism) is definitely not the only side of her mediating activity, nor is it the most important or primary one but only a consequence of her position within the plan of salvation. This does not, of course, mean that she should be swept aside or underrated. Prayerful and reverent meditation on Mary in her essence leads faith to an understanding of her God-given role within salvation. This leads further to imitation

of Mary's role whereby the individual becomes better disposed for participating in the work of Christ.

When emphasis has been placed only on the moral and
ascetical aspects, Marian piety has become one-sided and exaggerated. It has sketched a picture of Mary in which her
features were not objectively drawn and which consequently lacked authenticity and conviction. The devotional
response, as a consequence, is limited but not completely
vitiated. Devotion to Mary does not mean imitating her life
step by step. After all, we know so little about her life. But
her example is important and her basic attitude should be
copied by every Christian. Mary is the Archetype of the
primordial Christian. If man tries to dispose himself subjectively and personally to co-perform the work of Christ
and receive the fruits as Mary did, he will reach a much
more vivid sharing of life with Christ through Mary. The
graces Christ gained for us by His Sacrifice will be given
to him through the Church in fuller measure.

There is a final question connected with this exposition.
Actually it now can no longer be called a question at all.
We refer to the problem of the universality of graces imparted by Mary. Mary assumes the work of Christ by her
receptive co-redemption and accordingly receives the
fruits of this work for the Church. Universality is thereby
established. Mary's grace-giving, pictured imaginatively
as her supplication before Christ, is nothing more than the
extension of her co-redemptive mediatorship. It is universal
and without exception. There is no point where any graces
can be excluded from this mediatorship, not even the sacramental ones. We receive the sacramental graces as a result
of the power inherent in the sacramental sign. The sacra-

ment produces grace because grace has been given to it in and through Mary in the same way that it is given from and through the Church. In the mystery of salvation, during the administration of a sacrament, the Church is merely doing in the time-space dimension what Mary did for the Church as its representative: that is, assuming Christ's sacrifice and co-offering it interiorly as her own. Because Mary received Christ's *pleroma* of grace for the Church, she also received the grace contained in the sacraments and this grace flows from the *pleroma* into the sacramental sign and is given to the person to whom the sacrament is administered. Thus, if we must imagine Mary's mediation as a series of single acts of intercession, we should not hesitate to say that through her intermediary work she co-operated with Redemption, and also that a given sacramental sign contains sacramental grace. Benedict XV said: "For this reason (because of Mary's union with the suffering of her Son) all graces received from the treasury of Redemption are given to us through the hands of the Sorrowful Mother."[22]

Just as we cannot exclude any graces, neither can we exclude any individuals to whom graces are not imparted by Mary. There are no men who obtain grace without Christ and His Church. "Outside the Church there is no salvation" nor grace for any man. Even when a man is not in visible union with the Church, his participation in the life of Christ takes place through the Church and he is joined to this life-giving community by an invisible bond. But the Church's grace was first received by Mary and continues to flow from her into the Church and its members. Any restriction of Mary's intermediary function would also restrict the universality of Christ's mediation and the universal necessity of salvation through the Church. Scheeben writes: "Mary's mediation has one thing in common with Christ. . . . It is not only an essential but also a universal kind of mediation which in some mysterious way embraces all people, goods, and interrelationships with God that fall within the range of Christ's mediation."[23]

Smith says that "the scope of Mary's heavenly mediation is determined by two factors—by the earthly merit and by the spiritual surrender of the individual."[24] If this is true then the universality of Mary's mediation is clear. It is precisely this thought that sees her as the Type of the grace-giving and co-redeeming Church. "And so it is immediately clear that there are no limits whatever to Our Lady's effective intercession. Earthly merit and spiritual surrender are fused in Mary. Her merit and her spiritual function toward men are one and the same. It is her function to merit all graces for men [we outlined earlier the proper way to understand this] because she is the co-redeemer of the human race."

NOTES

1. Protestant Argument against the Catholic Church. Quoted by Schueth, S.J., F.H., *Mediatrix* (Innsbruck, 1925), p. 100.
2. Rom. 8,19ff.
3. *Die Physiologie der Kirche* (Mainz, 1931), pp. 109ff.
4. *Adversus haereses* III, 25, 7. – MG 7, 971 A.
5. N. 63.
6. N. 65.
7. N. 64.
8. 2 Cor. 11,2.

9. Rom. 8,20.

10. Koester, H.M., *Die Magd des Herrn. Theologische Versuche und Ueberlegungen* (Limburg, 1947), p. 106.

11. September 15, before the Lessons of the Third Nocturn of Matins.

12. "Das Fundamentalprinzip der Mariologie," in: *Scientia Sacra* (Koeln-Duesseldorf, 1935), p. 254.

13. *Gloriosae Dominae* (1748).

14. MG 77, 992.

15. *Ad diem illum, ASS* 36 (1903–04), p. 452.

16. *Dogmatik* III, n. 1771.

17. Leo XIII, *Adjutricem populi, ASS* 28 (1895–96).

18. Hebr. 7, 25.

19. Leo XIII, *Octobri mense, ASS* 24 (1891–92), p. 196.

20. Leo XIII, *Jucunda semper, ASS* 27 (1894–95), p. 178.

21. *Die Magd des Herrn*, p. 329.

22. *Inter Sodalicia, AAS* 10 (1918), p. 182.

23. *Dogmatik* III, n. 1630.

24. Smith, G.D., *Mary's Part in Our Redemption* (New York, Kenedy, 1938), and translated by B. Erasmi, *Die Stellung Mariens im Heilswerk Christi* (Paderborn, 1947), p. 199.

THE STRUCTURE OF
THE MARIAN MYSTERY

III

Mary as Archetype
of the Co-Redeeming Church

III

CHAPTER 5

The Bridal Mother of God

"THE EYES OF ALL CREATION are justly directed toward thee, for in thee and through thee and from thee the merciful hand of the Almighty has created anew His entire creation."[1] These ringing words end one of St. Bernard of Clairvaux's expositions on Mary's divine motherhood. Here Mary's mediation of salvation is clearly seen as the inner meaning of her divine motherhood. Here Mary is seen as the Type of the Church of which it can also be said: "in her, through her, and from her" creation has been renewed.

The mystery of divine motherhood is certainly that one which surrounds Mary most intimately with glory. This mystery asserts itself so impressively that the others time after time have seemed to be derived from it. In the divine motherhood, Mary was given the most perfect opportunity to prefigure the Church in a co-redemptive way. In the eyes of her fellow creatures who venerate her, no one is as exalted as she to whom such intimate relationship with her Creator was given in the divine motherhood. Everyone knows how zealous the Church has always been in defending the truth of this mystery—both against any tendency to underemphasize physical motherhood with regard to Christ's humanity and also against any restrictions to the merely human level. Mary is the true *Theotokos*. If she were not the Mother of God, she would not be a true Type of the Church.

One unfortunate tendency in theology has laid stress on the Incarnation and Redemption as the personal, juridical achievement of one individual, the God-man. To the extent that this error has flourished, awareness of the unity between the divinely human Redeemer and His Mystical Body has diminished. The result has been that even the Incarnation itself has been understood one-sidedly, and the divine motherhood has accordingly emerged as the ultimate Mariological mystery and the basis of all other Marian privileges. The fact, is, however, that the divine motherhood can be understood in the inner meaning that God intended only if we look upon Christ as the whole Christ, and Redemption as the unfolding of mankind into the Church.

We need not emphasize that we have no intention of minimizing the divine motherhood. In this mystery Mary first manifested her role in Redemption as Archetype of the Redeeming Church. No other mystery can better demonstrate more convincingly that man's affirmative surrender to God's salvation is equal to his own redemption. But this does not mean that we should cease seeking the ultimate meaning of Mary's motherhood. Rather, our progress increases our realization of the supreme idea that dominates Mary—the fact that she is Archetype of the Church.

The Church's early tradition venerated the mystery of

the divine motherhood. In this tradition, however, the mystery is seen as being clearly rooted in Mary's higher task as Type of the Redeeming Church. Thus—without in any sense diminishing the splendor of the mystery—the divine motherhood should be treated here in the context of Mary's redemptive task. The greatness of the mystery of divine motherhood enables her to put her co-redemptive function into action and thus actually become the Type of the Church. The grace of the divine motherhood is certainly an effect of salvation. But above all it makes Mary a co-redeemer whose co-redemptive action itself has already been merited. The grace of the divine motherhood is given in virtue of Mary's archetypal function in the redeeming Church. Thus we rightly treat the mystery of divine motherhood in the light of the concept of Type of the Redeeming Church.

The co-redemptive function of the Church is receptive —a state of readiness for the coming of the covenant. But the covenant itself takes place, as it were, in two stages. First, there is the reception of the *Logos*, who by becoming man, desires to enter humanity. Mary is the Bride of the *Logos* and thus Bride of the Father. From the Father she receives the Son so that she can give birth to Him on earth. Next, the now Incarnate God wishes to offer from the midst of mankind His sacrifice of reconciliation. Mary as the Bride of Christ must take on this sacrifice so that humanity may conclude a covenant with Christ. Thus both stages of the covenant—namely, the reception of the *Logos* and the sacrifice of the Incarnate God—are fulfilled in virtue of Mary's divine motherhood.

The Bride of the Logos

A characteristic sign of early Christian Mariology is its contemplation of Mary's function at the Annunciation and therefore at the Incarnation of the *Logos*. Her co-sacrifice through her co-suffering at the Cross receives little or no consideration. This should cause no surprise. It is a logical development, because early tradition does not limit Christ's saving work to the moral element of the sacrifice of reparation. This element is, in fact, even subordinate to the mystery of the ontological union between God and mankind at the Incarnation. The Incarnation by itself constitutes an element of Redemption. Therefore, the moral work of sacrificial submission to the Father—which culminates at the Cross—is complementary to the ontological union of God and mankind. Thus it is that the Fathers delight in praising and describing Mary's receptive capacity as co-redeemer as this capacity is exemplified in the *fiat* she pronounced at the Annunciation.

We call Christ's work Redemption. Actually this term is not completely adequate because it was not God's intention to save us from sin alone. Redemption, furthermore, should not be considered only in terms of the sacrifice on the Cross. This would relegate the Incarnation to the position of simply making Redemption possible. Some idea of the insufficiency of this view of Christ's work can be seen in the lack of complete understanding of what really happened at the Cross. Some presentations imply that satisfaction and reparation for sin were the only reasons for Christ's death. Actually, the main reason was the sacrifice itself; its worshipful surrender to the Will of the Father. Reparation is only a negative—though very important—element, because surrender and submission imply revocation and reparation of a previous rebellion. Even if these two elements were taken for granted, however, Christ's "Redemption" would not convey its complete meaning unless the essential union of humanity and divinity in the Incarnation were included. God's *Logos* penetrated mankind as a whole at the Incarnation, and humanity thereby became enlivened with Divine Life. But the essential union between God and man is insufficient in itself. The moral union—highlighted by Christ's surrender of His human Will to His Father—must be added. This is true because mankind, although hypostatically united to Divinity, was left untouched in its free, self-determining nature. The ontological union must be seconded by a moral union.

Thus we see that it is impossible to restrict Redemption—which divinizes mankind—to either one of these elements alone, if it is to be understood in its fullest sense. Emphasis on reparation and Christ's sacrifice on the Cross as the single "capital" element would be one-sided and incorrect. Equally one-sided and erroneous would be any exclusive concentration on the "mystical-physical" event of the Incarnation. Both are complementary elements belonging to the one wholeness of man's divinization. Characteristic of all saving and divinizing events is the collaboration between God and man. Within the divine-human framework God's part is the Incarnation, a purely divine act. God's own action (in collaboration between Divinity and humanity) is first and most important. Man's action is

mere response. Thus, within Redemption it is God's act
which is the most important part of the ontological and hypostatic union between Divinity and humanity. Even here
God's act would not have its redeeming effect if Christ's
human Will did not respond to it. The culmination of this
co-operation was the surrender on the Cross, the sacrifice
of reparation, that at the same time made man's own divinization morally meritorious.

Thus, when we attempt to see in Mary the receptively
co-operating Church we must seek this co-operation in
both elements of Redemption. If the entrance of the *Logos*
into humanity means that divine life has penetrated into
sin-ladened mankind, then humanity—embodied in Mary
—must also play a redemptive and co-redeeming part,
just as Mary (by assuming the work of the Redeemer on
the Cross) represented the Church beneath the Cross. In
this regard there is a danger of imposing a rigid simplifica-
tion of Mary's role. Not all authors have avoided this. On
the other hand Mary's co-operative role at the Incarnation has been treated as nothing more than preparation and
therefore as only indirect co-operation in the Redemption.
This error is due to considering the Redemption in a one-
sided way—simply as the satisfactory, meritorious work of
the Redeemer dying on the Cross. Lennerz writes, for example: "Mary co-operated physically so that the Incarnation could take place. It must therefore be said that she
co-operated formally and indirectly with Christ's redeeming actions, through free consent in the physical order."[2]
One would expect this of Lennerz because his idea of Redemption rests solely on the moral act which Christ per-

formed on the Cross. Lennerz writes further: "The Incarnation is not Christ's redemptive work."[3] It is of course true that the Incarnation is not the complete redemptive work of Christ and demands the moral surrender to God's Will as a completing factor. However, it is incorrect to assert that the Incarnation is not Redemption. Deneffe (who otherwise is always in extreme disagreement with Lennerz) is practically in agreement with him in this context. When speaking on *cooperatio in redemptione* in his thesis on Mary's role as mediator, he treats only of her co-operation in the Crucifixion. He excludes her co-operation at the Incarnation to the extent that he separates it as a first part from a second.[4]

On the other hand, Mary's co-operation at the Incarnation is sometimes treated as immediate co-operation at the Redemption. She goes forth as Bride of the *Logos* and utters her fiat to Him as He comes to redeem mankind. She participates with Redemption through this union. But here her part at the Redemption seems to be off center also. Her equally important work at the Crucifixion of the God-man is overlooked. And overemphasis of Mary's part as Bride of the *Logos* leads to overlooking the fact that even after the Incarnation Mary represents the Church as the Bride of the God-man, Christ.

The Fathers praised Mary for her role in the Incarnation as "cause of our salvation."[5] Her work consisted of direct co-operation in the sense we have proposed previously. If this is so this co-operation could be nothing less than the end result of redemptive grace. And—further—if this is so, then Mary did presuppose the work of the Redemption as a completed entity—not in the temporal order, of course, but in the logical and intentional order. The other position would be to consider Mary's activity as preceding the completed work of the Redemption. Then there would be a question only of indirect co-operation, a setting-up of a purely objective mechanism which has nothing to do with the essence of Redemption. The kind of co-operation we are discussing is receptive to, and influenced by, the effect of grace. Nevertheless, it is a *direct* co-operation with Redemption.

If we are to analyze the elements in the process of Redemption in their rational and causal structure, we must do so in the following manner. First, we must consider Christ's work in the ontological element of the hypostatic union between Divinity and humanity at the Incarnation. We must also consider the moral element of His expiation and meritorious submission to the sacrifice of the Cross, all entirely completed and terminated. This work which redeems mankind is the exclusive work of Christ Himself, Christ alone. The union between the human and divine natures is the work of the Creator Himself. The sacrificial work of the Crucifixion emerges from the midst of humanity and is solely the work of the God-man who offers it for mankind. The second factor to be considered is the following: the taking up of this work by mankind, which, as the Church, is represented by Mary, the Type of the Church. The Church embraces Redemption in both elements. She receives in Mary's grace "because of the pre-envisioned merits of Christ" the *Logos* into her midst. It is Mary who utters the *fiat* "for the whole of mankind."[6] Error is to be avoided here, too. We do not intend to imply that Mary represented a mankind without grace and had to say her *fiat* before grace could come. This position would be semi-Pelagian. Rather, the point here is that Christ's work was seen by God as completed. (In this development temporal sequence is of as little importance as it is in the Immaculate Conception.) But since Christ's work is seen by God as completed, mankind, co-operating with redemptive grace, has to assume the work of approaching the God of Redemption subjectively. Mankind does this in Mary. Tradition teaches it. Here she fulfills her task as Type of the Church. She does it primarily in the one ontological element inherent in the redemptive union of God and man in the Incarnation. But this implies participation with the other essential element of Redemption, Christ's sacrifice. This we will discuss in the next section.

Precisely because Mary is the Mother of God, she typifies mankind's relationship to the *Logos*, mankind which by its *fiat* to the coming of the *Logos* and His work becomes the Church. Here it is very important to remember that when the Church disputed with early Christian heresies she was never content to stress a solely physical motherhood for Christ's humanity. In the depths of her bosom the Church guarded the conviction that Mary was the Mother of God in the truest possible sense; it was from this point that the bell of mankind's *fiat* to the redemptive advent sounded forth. As Peter Chrysologus said so beautifully in a passage previously quoted: The Angel of God is like a bridal messenger of God who came to receive the consent of the human partner. Mary's *fiat*, the *fiat* of mankind, was

important to God—in a certain sense even necessary for
Redemption because Redemption establishes a relationship
between man and God which must be sealed at both extremes by a personal, free decision.

The *fiat* made Mary the Bride of the *Logos*. This becomes even clearer and more unique when we realize that
she pronounced it as His Mother. The *fiat* takes on a physical form in the flesh of the *Logos* that she contributed—
from man's side—to the Incarnation. This proves in an extremely clear way that the co-operation was receptive. The
individual human nature of the *Logos* was fashioned directly by Mary from the flesh of mankind. Thus, the ontological union of Divinity and humanity extends the possibility of participation to all men. Insofar as they participate
in Mary's receptive, ready, consenting co-redemption, the
Church has been realized in them.

Our statement here that Mary is the Bride of the *Logos*
is actually what tradition means when it is said that she is
Bride of the Father from whom she receives the Son so that
she might bear Him as God-man on earth. Our exposition
has perhaps made the doctrine even clearer.

The part played by mankind and represented and typified by Mary does not cause, provoke, or produce co-
operation with the work of Redemption. It is mainly a receptive opening-of-self—influenced by redeeming grace—
for the redemptive union of God and man. That is why
Mary's co-operation (typical of the Church's receptivity to
Redemption) took place in her motherhood when she received the *Logos* for the sake of humanity. The words of
the Church are very fitting in this context: Christ indeed

was not conceived in Mary through man lest the initiative and active co-operation be relegated to the human side. Mary conceived Christ through the Holy Spirit. It is God alone whose role in this element of Redemption is the primary and active one. We call it the ontological role, the mystical-physical union which attained perfect realization in the God-man and extended itself by grace into the Church where individuals are justified.

In the regular cycle of the Church's year, we celebrate Advent, or the recollection of the Incarnation and birth of the God-man. We also celebrate Mary's motherhood in a way that stresses our own involvement on a level that is truly redemptive—not merely a level of a pre-condition for Redemption. In the unfolding of this liturgy—but of course not only then—the Church pronounces repeatedly the same *fiat* uttered by Mary as Bride of the *Logos*. The individual believer repeats the *fiat* spoken by Mary as Type of the Church when he genuflects at the *Credo* in recognition of the Incarnation, and also, when he says the Angelus. He pronounces the *fiat* for the advent of the *Logos* to humanity so that his humanity may become divine. In the same way, when he receives grace through a sacrament (or through some other way), he again disposes himself for the effect of that grace. Thus, he co-operates redemptively with God whose coming to man through grace is his redemption.

It is therefore clear that Mary's divine motherhood is based on her position as the Type of the Church which receives Redemption. Mary, the Mother of Christ, has really become the Bride of the *Logos* with whom she made the saving covenant through her *fiat* as the bridal Mother of God, as the Archetype of the Church which is the Bride of the *Logos*.

The Bride of Christ

It must be stressed that Mary, the Type of the Church, is not only the Bride of the *Logos* or of the Father. Even after the Incarnation she typifies the Church in her bridal and receptive co-operation with the work of the God-man. Therefore Mary is also the Bride of Christ. Christ the God-man performs His sacrifice as the Head of humanity. He is the Man according to whose likeness all men were created. He is the new peak of humanity. As such He stands sacrificing before the Father. This, however, is not sufficient. If Christ is to offer His sacrifice as the representative of humanity, if this sacrifice of the God-man is also to be the sacrifice of humanity itself, He must certainly be chosen by humanity to be its own representative. Humanity must stand behind Him and make the sacrifice its own. The God-man's solidarity with humanity should be acknowledged not only by God the Father who accepts it; it must also be accepted by the men for whom He offers Himself. The task in all its essentials, the sacrificial union with and in Christ, is extended by the Church in time and space by the fact that she always declares Christ's sacrifice to be her own in her very administration of her sacramental and divine services. Moreover, in every subjective act performed by the individual believer, the Church assumes the work of Christ.

Only to the extent that the Church so acts does Christ's redemptive sacrifice become truly and actually effective. Therefore—though the Church is receptive—she is really co-redeemer.

The Church became co-redeemer in the first and final instance in Mary. She stood beneath the Cross and merited, in the words of Pius X, *"de congruo* what Christ merited *de condigno."*[7] Mary assumes the meritorious and sacrificial work of Christ entirely complete and terminated in itself. It was not by chance that the word used in this papal document is in the perfect tense in Latin. The expression is *Maria promeruit* rather than *de congruo promeret.* She takes it into her own heart and into the heart of the Church. She receives the fruit which Christ merited through His sacrifice. Through this receptive co-operation (uniting the God-man Christ and His work in Mary) the Church becomes the Bride of Christ. But there is no lessening of His position as the representative and sacrificing Head of humanity. Here, too, mankind's decision is essential. By it Christ is able to perform the sacrifice as Head of humanity. By it His sacrifice brings Redemption to mankind. But any decision which one person makes for or against another person and his work places him in confrontation with the other. Thus, the Church confronts the God-man in Mary. Her consent roots the decision in her very heart and receives the graces that make humanity the living Church.

The preceding paragraphs make clear that Mary's bridal relationship to the God-man cannot place her beside Christ in the same way that a bride would naturally stand beside her spouse. Mary has to remain completely receptive and

raised from this passivity only by Christ's grace. Christ,
and He alone, is the One who sacrifices and redeems. This
is why we refuse to call Mary a Priestess. If she were a
Priestess she would emerge as a co-sacrificing principle beside Christ. Actually she simply took into her own heart the
sacrifice consummated by Christ Himself in its moral and
subjective completion. This point may well have been in
question when the Holy Office decreed: "Pictures of the
Blessed Virgin in priestly garb should not be tolerated."[8]
The reason for this prohibition was made still clearer in a
letter sent by Cardinal Merry del Val to the Bishop of Ad-
ria in the reign of Pius XI. An article had been printed in
the Bishop's diocese in favor of the veneration of the *Virgo
Sacerdos*. Cardinal del Val's letter insisted that the Bishop
"inform the editorial staff that this veneration could not be
tolerated, according to the decree of the Holy Office of
April 8, 1916, and that it should not be permitted to be
propagated." This incident does not mean that "the Holy
Office had repudiated the official spread and veneration of
the title among the faithful for reasons of prudence, with
no reference to the theological idea as such."[9] The prohibition most likely had a solidly grounded reason—precisely
the fact that the title placed Mary beside Christ in a manner
that violates theological truth. It is possible to speak of
Mary's priestly function in the sense of participation, because obviously the whole Church and every individual believer takes on Christ's Priesthood. A believing Christian, as
a member of the Church, assumes Christ's sacrifice and has
a part in the fruits that follow. It is at this juncture that
Mary is so obviously the Type of the Church in de la
Taille's thought. He writes:

[Christ] allowed the entire Church to participate with His priesthood by making us here on earth into donors, subject to Him, who offer the sacrificial gift, which He in Heaven has perfected through His eternal glory. Therefore Christ chose the whole Church to be His co-redeemer insofar as we alone can gain the blessing of Redemption by co-offering its Price. The more the Church is redeemed, the more she is co-redeemer because she receives no fruits of salvation above what she gains for herself.[10]

Now let us bind both points together. The receptive bridal co-operation with Christ's work must become a reality. Simultaneously the integral uniqueness of Christ's position must be visibly emphasized. God found the solution to the two polarities in Mary's motherhood. She is a human being whose tender bonds of maternal relationship to her Child enable her to co-experience her Son's work deep within her being. She assumes it and accordingly becomes united to Him as a loving bride. On the other hand, however, the bridal relationship in any usual sense does not disturb Christ's unique position. It is precisely Mary's position as the Mother of God that enables these two essential elements—inherent in her co-redemptive role as Type of the Church—to become reality. Mary is able to typify the Church as the Bride of Christ, the God-man of sacrifice, and not displace Him while standing beside Him.

In the binding together of these two elements a favorite thought of the Fathers—especially St. Augustine—finds fulfillment: Mary receives the fruits of the Church from her Bridegroom-Son by co-performing His sacrifice bridally and in her own soul; because of this she is physically (in the supernatural sense of the word) and spiritually the Mother of Christ's entire Mystical Body. Into that Body she pours forth her Son's *pleroma*. At this juncture, moral receptive co-operation with the moral element in Christ's redemption—founded in the mystical-physical element of the Incarnation—is completed. When Mary conceived the God-man, she became ontologically the Mother of the Mystical Christ. This element had to receive the addition of moral completion at Christ's sacrifice on the Cross. Mary's participation in both elements is possible through her divine motherhood.

Thus, we see that Mary's task as the Type of the Church is fulfilled because she is the Mother of God. But she became the Mother of God because she was destined to be the Archetype of the Church, the Bride of the *Logos* and of Christ.

NOTES

1. St. Bernard, *Sermo* 2 *de Pentec*, n. 4. – ML 183, 328 B.
2. "De redemptione et cooperatione in opere redemptionis," in *Gregorianum*, 22 (1941), p. 313.
3. *Loc. cit.*, p. 313.
4. Pesch, Chr., *Compendium theologiae dogmaticae*, t. II. Additamentum propositio XXIa (Freiburg, 1940), p. 299.
5. Irenaeus, *Adversus haereses* III, 22, 4. – MG 7, 959 A.
6. St. Thomas, *S. th.* III, q.30, a.1.
7. *Ad diem illum, ASS* 36 (1903–04), p. 449ff.
8. Decree of April 8, 1916. – *AAS* 8 (1916), p. 146.
9. Seiler, S.J., H., *Corredemptrix* (Rome, 1939), p. 27.
10. *Mysterium fidei* (Paris, 1924), p. 648. Eng. trans., *Mystery of Faith* (New York, Sheed and Ward, 1930).

CHAPTER 6

The Virginal Bride of Christ

Virginal Mother

From earliest times in the history of dogma, Mary's divine motherhood and her virginity were brought sharply and closely together as the focal point in disputations. This most probably was not the result of chance, and the Church soon distinguished the difficult dogma into the two concepts of *Theotokos* and *Aeiparthenos,* thus giving ample substance to the ancient proverb that Mary alone is the conquerer of all heresies on earth. Through this twofold mystery, Mary was interwoven into the warp and woof of the arguments revolving around Christological dogma. The concepts of her divine motherhood and her virginity were simultaneously rooted deeply in ecclesiastical tradition. Her true motherhood of God was a fact that the earliest apologists defended rigorously against the Gnostic heresies. They similarly defended the fact that she was and remained a Virgin. With very few exceptions, ecclesiastical tradition always tenaciously held the concept that Mary is *aei parthenos.* (The most notable exception is found in many passages in Irenaeus which, if taken out of context, leave some doubt whether he explicitly taught that Mary was a Virgin in all the usually quoted stages of her life—*ante, in et post partum Christi.*)

The Church did not declare the permanence of Mary's Virginity in what could be termed the inductive way. Theologians did not first establish the fact in one stage, then another, etc. For example: Was she a Virgin before the birth; Was she a Virgin during the birth; Was she a Virgin after the birth? If this had been the process the concept of *aei* would have been derived from the sum total of the arguments. Rather, Mary's permanent virginity was a certainty simply accepted as a revealed fact, even though it could be easily explained by her position in the history of salvation. The parallel between Christ and Adam in the economy of salvation demands the parallel between Mary and Eve and also between Mary and the still virginal earth from which Adam was formed. Thus her virginity can be explained even after it has been accepted as a fact of Revelation. The Early Church had to battle various heresies that denied either Christ's true divinity or His true coming into human flesh, both of which minimized the saving bridal bond between God and man. The Fathers were forced to stress the validity of both the human and the divine natures and establish the true bridal relationship of Mary to the Redeemer as Mother of God, who, because of her virginity, is not bound to any human being. The early Christian apologists strove to demonstrate this aspect of salvation in their Mariology. Tertullian, for example, states emphatically: "Just as Christ became man through the Holy Spirit and the Virgin Mary, we should all be reborn through the Holy Spirit and the Virginal Church, the Mother of us all."[1]

We have acknowledged that Mary's motherhood of
Christ is the mystery through which her position as Type
of the Church was to be realized within the economy of
salvation. No mystery could more accurately prefigure the
receptive, co-redemptive Church than that of Mary, the
Mother of God, who opened a gateway for the *Logos* to
enter humanity and gather men around Him in the Church.
And the Church, in turn, roots Christ's sacrifice into her
very being. Nothing can better sum up and symbolize this
Church than Mary beneath the Cross. By her motherly co-
suffering she roots Christ's sacrifice into her heart and
thereby becomes the maternal beginning of the Church's
life.

It is in the context of the above development that Scheeben calls the divine motherhood bridal. Mary accepted the
Logos through her maternal receptivity; she contributed
the bodily substance for His Incarnation. Ecclesiastical tradition never ceases to stress that she was the first one asked
and that she did it freely through her *fiat*. That is why
Mary appears as a bride in her motherhood. Even if Mary
had not known at the Annunciation that the Incarnation of
God was involved, the essence of her divine motherhood
would not be touched. Her *fiat* to God's plans would have
been sufficient in any case. When—according to tradition
—the Church came forth from the dying Second Adam
(just as Eve came forth from the side of the sleeping first
Adam), it was because the *pleroma* of redemptive grace
came down upon Mary beneath the Cross and transformed
her into the germ of the Church that was born from the
side of the dying Christ. Even here Mary's divine motherhood stands out clearly as bridal. Her inner empathy and

compassion enabled her to take her Son's sacrifice for herself and for the Church.

Mary's divine motherhood is virginal as a result of this receptivity. In the plan of salvation, Mary as Mother and Type of the Church does not stand before or above, but at the side of, Christ. Her motherhood is not determined by man. It is virginal and became fruitful through the Breath of the Holy Ghost. In the Church virginity is never negative and empty, but rather a filling with the love for Christ which more than any worldly love demands the focus of the whole human being. Similarly—in Mary's virginity— her freedom from any human tie is the result of her attachment to Our Lord and His work. With Mary God shows Himself as "the jealous God,"[2] the way He appeared in the Old Testament in His contact with His Chosen People and as He wishes to be and must be toward His people of the New Testament—the Church. Mary, the Type of the Church, is at the command of the jealous God with whom, in representing the Church, she made the holy bridal covenant which brought redemption to her and to the whole Church.

Mary's motherhood of Christ does not in any way make a bridal relationship to another human being impossible or even difficult. Theologians, of course, constantly try to base her virginity upon her divine motherhood. The fact of her virginity was established by Revelation and closely associated with her divine motherhood at a very early date and the relationship between the two concepts is so close that it seems logical to base one upon the other. It is also most natural that mankind's veneration of Mary should find her virginity a fitting state for the Mother of God. The theological reasoning behind this association can be followed only with considerable difficulty—a difficulty which we shall see has reasonable justification. The impression is far too strong, in discussions of this difficulty, that the marital bond is not suitable for the Mother of God, the holiest of all the saints. The idea creeps in that the marital bond is somehow inferior.

We too certainly insist that virginity is the only fitting state for the Mother of God. Our reasoning, however, is not based on the divine motherhood in itself. Rather, we affirm that Mary's bridal relationship to the *Logos* and to Christ was brought about by means of the divine motherhood. Both states therefore—divine motherhood and virginity—can be explained by a third point common to both: Namely, Mary, the Archetype of the Church, "is espoused to one Husband and consecrated as a chaste Virgin to Christ."[3] Thus, Mary's virginity is not a sort of limitless privilege cloaked around her without any inner meaning or even something contradictory. Naturally speaking, of course, simultaneous virginity and motherhood is a paradox. But in Mary's case this is not so because her motherhood is a bridal state and her bridal relationship to Christ demands virginity with regard to other human ties. If Mary had been united to a man in the human bridal manner, her bridal relationship toward the *Logos* and toward Christ would have become overshadowed, prejudiced and unclear. Mary's place in salvation is unlike that of any other member of the Church. The Church is bridally related to Christ. As Archetype, Mary clearly and purely expresses the essence of the Church which is the Bride of Christ. Thus, Mary had to be free of any bridal or nuptial ties toward any hu-

man. It is true that her virginity remained ambiguous during the early years of her life and at the beginning of
Christ's ministry. "Jesus was thought to be the son of Joseph."[4] Yet, this virginity had to emerge in its shadowless
brilliance at the moment the human reason for its veiling
ceased—when the Church began to grow as the image of
the virginal Mother. Thus, in the very first confessions of
faith the Church proclaimed Christ's birth from the *Virgin*
Mary.

Once the title Virgin-Mother was established, the concepts of Mary and the Church became indissoluble in the
minds of the faithful. The Church is a mother. But she is
free from heresies and earthly ties. She must be so because
she is the bride of Christ, her Redeemer. Mary is a mother.
She could not become attached to any man in marriage because "her work belongs to the King." From one point of
consideration—as Bride of the *Logos* and Christ—Mary
appears not in a natural bridal relationship to Christ but as
His mother, in whose inner person the attitude of bride was
realized. From the opposite point of view, Mary's motherhood is not such that it could deprive her of the liberty
with which she offered her spirit, heart, and body to Christ.
No hostility toward marriage or contempt of things sex-
ual caused the Early Church's emphasis on Mary's virginity. Proof of this is found in the fact of the Church's
clear definition of the doctrine during the battle with
Gnosticism. As the Second Eve, Mary had to stand before
Christ as the Virgin-Bride. She was virginally free from
every man and virginal toward Christ. She could never be
Christ's bride in any human sense because this would have
marred the singularity of His position as Redeemer.

The Virginal Church

We have seen that as Type of the Church Mary must be a virgin. Since this idea has been emphasized from earliest times, we will now have to clarify some rather vague and doubtful points. There is no ambiguity in the Fathers' thought on this function of Mary in the history of salvation. It was understandable that they should regard Mary as a perpetual virgin in all the phases of her life where virginity might possibly be put in jeopardy. Later theology called this virginity *ante partum, in partu et post partum Christi*. Contrary to H. Koch,[5] it can be affirmed that "Tertullian, as a Montanist, was the first and only writer (until the time when St. Jerome sharply repudiated Helvidius) who denied Mary's perpetual virginity."[6]

The Church is the Bride of Christ. Her essence as the Mystical Body of Christ means that as a community of personal human beings, she maintains her bridal, loving moral union with Christ, her Bridegroom. It means she assents to His work. It means that she receives the fruits of His work, the intimate sharing of mystical-physical life. It is in this reception that the Church as Mystical Body is perfected. As a result, the Church belongs to Christ exclusively and this is a characteristic of her inner substance despite her unfaithfulness testified by history. This inner faithfulness is essential because God's guidance could never permit her essence to be destroyed or her essential features to be disfigured. The exclusiveness of the Church's love for Christ, her Bridegroom, is based on the fact that her bridal union with Him is the reason for her continuing existence. Under the guidance of the Holy Spirit, the Spirit of love, the

Church in her innermost being and amid her sharpest battles has clung consciously to this idea, like a bride feeling the continuing experience of her love. Let us cite some examples. The Gnostic and Manichean heresies tried to deprive the Church of one of her essential elements and snatch away her surrender to the Bridegroom. These heresies declared matter to be evil, and, by denying human freedom, made the bridal covenant between the Church and Christ impossible. In the fight against naturalistic Pelagianism, man alone was important, thus leaving no room for a saving covenant with God. Similarly, in the controversy with the semi-Pelagians. Here the human *fiat* is given the exaggerated role as the one condition for the coming of the *Logos* and His grace. In all these battles the Church defended her knowledge of her bridal relationship to Christ. She also fought for her virginal relationship as His bride. This is proved in her efforts to banish sinful love and sinful earthly attachments whenever these threatened to disfigure or weaken the Church in her continuing fight to preserve her virginal-bridal role.

The Church's only role in the history of salvation is the affirmation of Christ's work. As a bride she looks upon His work and tries to imitate Him in devout veneration. Therefore Pius X's thoughts on Mary can be applied equally well to the Church and we can use his statement to explain the Church because it is true of Mary: "Because of the sharing of suffering and willing between Mary and Christ, Mary merited and was able to become truly the regenerator of this corrupt earth; consequently she became the dispenser of all the gifts that Jesus gained for us by His bloody death."[7] If we were to substitute "the Church" for "Mary" in Pius' statement, the logic would not be changed.

To the extent that the Church turns away from anything opposed to God, the more her dedication to Christ and His work (her bridal acceptance and confirmation) becomes reality. The Church must be free for Christ; she must be virginally free. She will be so the more she brings her own essence into fulfillment. Mary the Archetype perfects the Church's essence and that is why she remained a Virgin throughout her life, *aei parthenos*. That is also why people who choose virginity in the Church have always been specially honored since earliest times. The Church, of course, does not think that all people should be virgins. Virginity certainly is not an ideal state for everyone. But those who do remain virgins for the sake of forming a [special] living bond with Christ express the Church's essence in a distinct way and let it shine as a special light within their surroundings.

Virginity became a firmly established state very early and the vows symbolize the permanency which is of the very fibre of the Church. Virginity is not a purely pragmatic state, leaving greater freedom for the ministry and for apostolic works, although such an advantage can be included in and be the result of the original intent. Virginity is an element which was and had to be expressed by Mary, the Virgin of virgins, in a typical way as its primordial image. She is the Archetype of the Church in the fullest sense: thus she is free from ties of creature love for the sake of her bridehood with Christ (which forms the essence of the whole Church with all her individual members participating). If an individual, due to a special calling, is designated to express the Church's essence in his own life, he must stand firmly before Christ with the exclusive love that the bridal bond demands of him; he must stand before all other men with the liberty which is meant to be used for all. A person bound to Christ in this special way receives graces for himself and for those around him; particular tasks of salvation are assigned him which send him out toward other men. Mary prefigured the state of being bound to Christ and sent out to men which is so characteristic of the Church. Consequently she fulfilled her freedom in a special way. This was, of course, when, miraculously, she was a virgin before, during and after the birth of Christ, her Bridegroom, *aei parthenos.*

NOTES

1. *De carne Christi,* ch.17 – ML 2, 826f.
2. Deut., 6,15
3. 2 Cor., 11, 2.
4. Luke 3, 23.
5. *Virgo Eva – Virgo Maria* (Berlin, 1937).
6. Niessen, J., *Die Mariologie des hl. Hieronymus* (Muenster, 1913), p. 26.
7. *Ad diem illum.*

IV

Mary, the Archetype of
the Redeemed Church

CHAPTER 7

Redemption of the Soul

Redemption from Original Sin

"This is a great mystery, I mean in Christ and His Church. When Christ entered His city He found her unclean, miserable, and blood-stained. He washed her, anointed her, fed her, and then clothed her in a garment beautiful beyond comparison. After He had become her very robe, He led her to Heaven where her inheritance was waiting."[1] In these words St. John Chrysostom states that the Church comes into being the moment she is free from original sin. The city to which Christ comes is humanity, into whose midst the Lord entered through His Incarnation. He found her unclean and miserable. He healed her by transforming her into the Church. Humanity is the Church to the extent that she has received salvation through Christ's sanctifying touch. The Church is nothing more than a community of redeemed men, to the extent that they have been redeemed.

The Church is the mysterious Body of Christ. It throbs with divine Life and bestows this Life upon all members who are vitally united to Him. Man's physical and spiritual components must both be drawn into the Church because the physical also is destined for Redemption. No one ceases to belong to the Church as long as he belongs physically to its organization, even though he may no longer be filled with the life of grace. On the other hand, a man who through no fault of his own does not belong to the visible organization can be vitally united to the Lord's Mystical Body and therefore be considered, in a sense, a member of the Church. Neither of these points, however, probes the essence of the Church as a community of redeemed men. The fact remains that man is redeemed to the extent that he belongs to the Church and that he belongs to the Church to the extent that he is redeemed.

To be redeemed means to be filled with Christ's life; it means a sharing of life with the Triune God. Therefore, it means release from inherited, original sin which separates man from the source of life. When man becomes incorporated into the Mystical Body, separation ceases, because this Body is unalterably dedicated to the Father. It cannot turn for a second toward any creature if such would imply disregarding the Father, with whom Christ lives inseparably united in loving unity with the Holy Spirit. Incorporation into Christ contradicts the state of original sin. If, therefore, the Church is man redeemed in Christ, she was orientated toward God the Father the moment she came into being. Her sign is the shining mirror by which Aberkios[2] symbolized her as belonging to God and not to the Devil.

Accordingly the Church must be free of original sin in its very essence from its first moment of existence, if this essence is existence in Christ as His Mystical Body. The Church must be the one conceived without original sin. In the maternal womb of humanity, estranged from God and burdened with the guilt of the first parents, the Church was conceived—without original sin.

If this is true, can the Church be personified by a figure who is not similarly without original sin? Here we do not mean deliverance from original sin after having been burdened. No. The Church, whose essence is to be free of original sin, could be personified only by a figure who from the very first moment of her existence was conceived immaculate, without original sin. This quality has to be a truly essential mark of that figure. Thus we praise the fact that Mary was conceived immaculately as her characteristic sign. No other Marian privilege, except for the virginal motherhood, has been repeated and emphasized more frequently than the Immaculate Conception.

The first and obvious purpose of an archetype is to personify something. Consequently, it must be able to clarify the spiritual reality underlying all the essential features of the object which it visibly represents. But we have seen that the Church's freedom from original sin is a note derived from her very essence. During the development of dogma, of course, there may have been times when a certain vagueness and uncertainty prevailed about Mary's conception without original sin. Thomas Aquinas apparently did not believe in the Immaculate Conception and held rather to her deliverance from sin in her mother's womb. Morgott's statement that Thomas implicitly taught the essence of the dogma does not seem very convincing.[3] Even so, in Thomas and the other Scholastics, a tendency to accept the mystery can be noticed. The fact that they did not acknowledge it fully—even though the divine motherhood was at the center of their Mariology—perhaps indicates clearly that the divine motherhood in itself is not the fundamental Marian mystery but only becomes basic when taken in the light of its archetypical significance.

Thus, the innermost essence of the Church is visibly and tangibly represented in Mary. Her figure proclaims that the Church is redeemed; that the redeemed Church is humanity, which Our Lord took and incorporated with Himself when this same Church went out to meet Him with her bridal *fiat*. In Mary conceived immaculately, the Church emerges as the one essentially redeemed, the one that could never exist tainted with original sin and therefore, in the womb of humanity, was conceived free from this sin. Mary's Immaculate Conception does not mean that she did not need salvation. She descended in a natural way from Adam and was burdened with the *debitum* of original sin. Even she could have been born with the stain of this sin if it had not been prevented on account of the "pre-envisaged merits of Christ." The same can be said of the Church for whom "Christ delivered Himself that He might sanctify her, cleansing her in the bath of water by means of the Word."[4] This comes about not as if there already were a Church laden with sin that first had to be cleansed. Just as Mary was preserved from original sin and conceived immaculate, the Church came into existence freed from original sin. Incorporation into the Church by the water of Baptism and freedom from original sin are identical events. Only the person who has been freed from original sin can be a member of the Church. Conversely, whoever is free from original sin realizes the Church within himself. Mary is the personification, the living figuration of the Church—absolutely without original sin because she is the one conceived without original sin through Christ's Redemption.

These interrelated points are buttressed by further considerations. Mary's personification of the Church that is free from original sin was not the product of an arbitrary imagination or the choice of a human mind, however profound. Mary personifies the Church because she is organically and realistically connected with it. In Mary the Church encounters Christ, her Bridegroom. In Mary the Church has said her *fiat* to the work of the Bridegroom. In Mary the Church has received her holiness and plenitude of graces. Ambrose says, "Mary has received the Redemption for all."[5] This "all" is the Church as a whole—not a collection of many individuals. The Church draws her plenitude of graces (which of course means freedom from original sin) from Mary, in whom all this fullness was deposited.

Thus, Mary is simply full of grace. The angel said this in his salutation because he added to the word *kaire* the name of her whom he addresses *kekaritomene*. Of course, Mary is redeemed in the same manner as the entire Church; that is, she is free from original sin only because of Christ's work. From the very first moment of her existence and in virtue of the pre-envisaged merits of Christ—together with the pre-envisaged ready consent in her own spirit—Mary received the plenitude of graces that kept her from original sin. In the temporal order, Mary's freedom from original sin may be put prior to the moment of her free consent and prior to the act by which she assumed the work of Christ

Himself. From the viewpoint of cause, however, her freedom from original sin depended upon her own *fiat*, her receptive co-operation.

The Church already existed in a very true, real sense at the first moment of Mary's life. She existed in those who were justified in the Old Covenant and in all people to whom grace had come and who were freed from original sin because of Mary's co-redemptive *fiat*. St. Bonaventure says, "When the fullest blessing was given to the Church through Mary, condemnation in its causality, guilt and punishment, was wiped out."[6] St. Bonaventure also said that "the fullness which was in Mary flowed into the whole Church." If this is true, the grace of Redemption must really dwell in Mary in all its fullness. It dwells within the fullness that fills Mary's whole being and her entire temporal life from the first moment she began to exist. This grace dwells within her because she is the Archetype and germ of the Church, which from the first moment of its existence was without original sin.

Redemption from Personal Sin

Among the many guideposts in Scripture that characterize the Church's essence and uniqueness we find the following statement by St. Paul: "Christ wished to present to Himself a Church brilliant with glory. He did not want her to have a spot or a wrinkle or anything of that nature, that she might be holy and without a blemish."[7] The statement is unrealistic at first glance. Scripture—especially the letters of St. Paul—realistically exposes the sins of the Church.

The unfailing truth of God's words should be proof indeed that St. Paul's statement is not a passing exaggeration nor a rhetorical aberration which should not be taken too seriously. Taken in context, Paul's words were meant to motivate the moral conduct of Christians by going to the root of Christian existence. Thus, the statement must be acceptable without reservation as characteristic of the Church's essence. Ecclesiastical tradition agrees with St. Paul when it stresses the Church's holiness as proof of her divinity. The First Vatican Council, also, when listing the properties that prove the Church's divinity, does not omit her essential holiness.[8]

The true meaning of St. Paul's words would certainly not be very clear to anyone who gives them only a passing glance. Such a person will point to the all-too-obvious unholiness of the Church. Emphasis will be placed on human failure found wherever the Church has come into being. He will ask, "Where is this holiness of the Church?" He will note the wrinkles in her face and not be satisfied with the dictum that "the glory of the King's daughter is within."[9] Rather, he will contrast this statement with St. Paul's which clearly stresses that wrinkles and spots have no place on the face of the Church. Inadequacies, faults, sinfulness and misery are all too obvious in a Church eager to maintain her essential visibility. Such a Church must reckon with the fact that these faults and sins are imputed to her as her own. The alibi of trying to escape these attacks by retreating into the Church's purely interior spiritual realms will not work. The Church is not a haphazard group that came together by chance. She is an essentially visible organization.

Furthermore, if we were to declare that the Church's holiness means that no sin can be found within her, we would be contradicting her own testimony about herself. The Church knows that her Founder drew sinners as well as the just into the orbit of His love; she knows that He did not permit the weeds to be rooted out of His growing, maturing field. "It is not the healthy who need a physician but those who are sick."[10] In these words Christ justified and explained His love for sinners—a love, of course, not understood by the self-righteous who encountered Him. The Church knows that she is the guardian of Christ's work; she knows that she has been sent into the world by the power of the same Christ. She knows that the same Christ continues to do His work in her; that then and now He was sent even more for men sick with sin than for the healthy. The Church fulfills her task by gathering human beings to herself and helping them—by sharing a common life-principle—to participate in Redemption. Thus, she must have sinners in her midst in order that they may receive life in her.

How has the Church defended herself against the misunderstanding of her sanctity? How has she answered the claim that she is a community of the sinless? The reaction has always been the same, whether it was in the time of Tertullian and St. Augustine, or in the struggle against the spiritualism of the Middle Ages, or in the quarrel with the Reformation of the sixteenth century. The Church has always, as it were, sided with the sinners and declared that she is their home, too. "One must not imagine that the Body of the Church, just because it bears the name of Christ, consists during the days of its earthly pilgrimage, only of members noted for their holiness; or that it is made up only of the group whom God has predestined to eternal happiness. It is the Savior's infinite mercy that allows place in His Mystical Body for those whom He did not exclude from the banquet of old."[11] This doctrinal assertion, most pertinent to our theme, is not new. It is found throughout the centuries in the ancient tradition of the Church.

St. Paul's words, therefore, should not be understood in a sense implying that only saints and sinless men are members of the Church. On the other hand, we cannot underestimate the statement (as we said before) and rob it of serious meaning by calling it rhetorical. The Church is holy with her innermost essence as the starting point. This holiness should not, however, be considered merely as an objective quality, the result of the ontological, objective union with God. It is also a moral and ethical holiness.

The essence of the Church, like the essence of any reality, can come into being in varying degrees. This is especially true when the realization does not depend on purely objective data alone but also upon the moral decision of free human beings. The essence of the Church (wherever it has been realized) does not attain the same degree of perfection in each of her members. The more this essence is attained, however, the more sin is removed and holiness is present. The very essence of the Church demands this. "Guilt is a contradiction of that which is the Church."[12]

The innermost essence of the Church means participation in Christ's Redemption. This takes place by men being "caught" by God; by their being rooted in Christ. It also means a taking hold of Christ's Redemption by those men in whom the Church is being established. Here is where the Church is receptively co-redemptive. To the extent that men participate in Christ's Redemption, they are the Church. To the extent that they are the Church, men participate in Christ's Redemption. In its truest sense, this redemption can only be fulfilled where the inner grace of a life in Christ (a vital participation in the life of the Triune God) is present and simultaneously finds visible expression in visible membership in the organized Church, actually its sacramental sign. The entire human being must take part in Redemption. Thus, man's corporeal nature must also be included, essentially and actively, in the Church. Union with the Church can be loosened by severance from the visible Church community. A weakening can also take place by loss of the Divine Life in which man participates because he lives within the divine-human community of the Mystical Body of Christ, the Church. "The sinner does not belong to the Church in the same full sense as the just. It is of primary importance to understand that we can and must speak of a membership in the Church covering all the directions and dimensions in which the Church has expanded. As a consequence, whoever does not belong to the Church in some one dimension cannot be counted as her member in the fullest sense."[13]

Thus, again, our definition of Redemption is not deliverance from sin alone; it is the bestowal of the life that exists in the Triune God. We, redeemed human beings endowed with grace, must co-enact the interior trinitarian life-process which, for us, is the most profound mystery of all. This can only take place when one of the three Divine Persons "implants" us in Himself in the vital unity that pervades our spiritual life, but of course does not infringe upon our status as individuals. The union that results from the Divine Life pulsating through our souls is so strong that the Fathers did not hesitate to call it divine. The union of those human beings who have been transplanted into a living community with the Incarnate *Logos* is the Mystical Body of Christ. They have been transplanted as whole men, body and soul. By reason of their unity they belong together because of their common sharing of Christ, and as members of a visible union, the Church.

Thus, the innermost essence of the Church contradicts sin, and sin contradicts the Church's essence. Sin, of course, exists everywhere that the Church has come into being. But the reality of the world is such that the Church cannot ever completely fulfill her essence anywhere. Men realize the Church's essence through a decision of the will. The Church, therefore, is always on the way toward fulfillment. The more the Church is fulfilled, the more sin is removed. "If both holiness and sin find a place in the Church's outward appearance, this certainly does not mean that in the Church they have the same relation to her hidden essence and thus belong to the Church in the same manner. . . . Sin remains a reality within her that contradicts her essence; her holiness is the revelation of her fundamental essence."[14] Karl Rahner correctly observes in the same essay that in any event "the Church is essentially an appearance, a sign of God's grace in the world; a sign made tangible through history." Sin in the "outward seeming" of the Church is therefore not something which exists only on the fringe or unessential part of the Church. It is of the very essence of the Church to be "outward seeming." But the following point must be maintained: Within the "outward seeming" of the Church, sin is a contradiction of her essence. This is so because to the extent that holiness exists (holiness meaning freedom from sin), the Church is realized.

Let us return to St. Paul's statement quoted at the beginning of this section. It would appear that we must not be too easily satisfied with the solution that being "without spot or wrinkle" is a state reserved for the Church in eternity. The statement has equal validity for the Church in her earthly pilgrimage. The Church comes into being simultaneously with her clearly defined and organized form when sin is removed. Hence the Church exists, is really present where and insofar as she is actually free from spots and wrinkles. But she will fulfill her "hidden essential reason" in its fullest sense when she enters into the perfection of eternity and where the Divine Life of Christ will pulsate within her without any hindrance or weakening.

We have seen and acknowledged that the basic principle of the Marian mystery is the fact that she is the Archetype and therefore the ideal type of the Church. The "essential reason" (lying hidden behind the Church's contradictory sinfulness on earth) shines forth unblemished in her as Archetype. She represents the Church as a true type, especially in the elements that are most invisible. Her task as representative is to bring into living, visible reality the essence of the Church hidden by the inevitability of sinful human nature. Above all, the following consideration must be made: If a reality is something that comes into being by a process of unfolding or development, if this unfolding also takes place both through the vital necessity of its essence and by a free decision of the will prompted by a representative figure; if all this is so—then the representative figure cannot express the essence of the thing incompletely or half-way. The representative Archetype must also be the ideal type; the personification has to be both model and moral example.

A further consideration: Mary is simply "full of grace" because of her task in salvation as Type of the Church. She was exempted from original sin from the first moment of her existence. Thus, the effect of her grace has to extend toward her deliverance from personal sin. This does not mean that her being Type of the Church and depository of all graces for the whole Church physically precluded her sinning. Her sinlessness is a metaphysical fact, not a physical impossibility. The exact way in which God's plenitude of graces made Mary's sinlessness possible (necessary, of course, because of her position as Archetype) brings up the problem of the tensions between grace and human freedom, which theologians have debated heatedly for centuries. Here it may be sufficient to affirm that Mary is Archetype in the manner of a cell. Since the entire plenitude of grace is implanted there, she has to be sinless by her very essence.

Here, more than from other viewpoints, Mary as Archetype becomes naturally a model and example, too. She is the model against whom the Church as a whole and all her members can examine their own attitude toward their redemption and fullness of grace as they work out their own lives. The individual Church-member's awareness of being the Church (a task to be accomplished by his own moral decision) must be seen as ontologically and morally perfected by Mary's ideal image and example. The Church living in her individual members needs Mary for her growth toward what she is and toward her hidden potential. Mary causes the essence of the Church to shine before individual human beings to appeal to their own moral efforts.

Thus, Mary has to be without sin from every viewpoint as Type of the Church. She has to be "without spot or wrinkle or any such thing," as St. Paul says of the Church. In Mary this essence of the Church is actually fulfilled. We do not need to wait until we reach eternity to find it. The Church has Mary as her peak and focal point and—contradictory as it might seem—as her actually existing ideal. It is Mary's task that the whole Church be formed according to her as Archetype, the fulfillment of its hidden essence.

From what we have said there should be no surprise that the Church's tradition again and again has taught the doctrine that Mary is free from sin. The Council of Trent clearly stressed the idea that she was exempted from the general law and burden of sin.[15] St. Augustine had taught the same doctrine a thousand years before. He wrote: "Suppose all the saints were standing before us and we asked them if they were without sin. All—with the exception of the Virgin Mary—would shout out in unison that such an assertion would be a delusion; that they would be liars to make such a claim. Note carefully the exception of the Virgin. When considering her, I will not even tolerate the question. We know she received more grace to conquer sin in every possible way. We know this because she was the one who merited to conceive and give birth to Him of whom it is certain that He was without sin."[16]

St. Thomas Aquinas has a very clear demonstration that Mary's sinlessness is not on the same level as that of other saints. The saints ascend gradually, he says. Mary's freedom from sin is based on her position in the salvation which embraces the whole Church. St. Thomas claims (if we may paraphrase his thought in modern terminology) that the other saints "specialize" in certain virtues, while Mary embraces them all. "She has performed the works proper to all virtues; other saints, by comparison, only certain ones. One was humble, another chaste, another charitable. Therefore they are meant to serve as examples for these particular virtues. But the Blessed Virgin is the model of all virtues."[17]

The Fathers, we know, preached Mary's freedom from sin. Later Patavius said: "No Catholic refuses to believe that Mary was untouched by the stain of sin, even the slightest."[18] We must not, however, understand this doctrine as a piling up of privileges expressed in wordy rhetoric that escapes rational investigation. The critical faculty of tradition has always been on guard in this mystery. Proof can be found in the Fathers, some of whose thinking came to different conclusions. For example, some thought they could find imperfections or even sin in Mary—we know this was the case with Tertullian, Origen, Basil, Cyril of Alexandria, Chrysostom, and even Ambrose. The Reformers of the sixteenth century gloated over these opinions. These Fathers were, however, solidly opposed by the rest of tradition on this subject. Patavius knew well and quoted the contradictory ideas in the Fathers and summed up by saying that Mary's freedom from sin was to be upheld as a certainty of faith.[19] The doctrine of Mary's freedom from sin is based upon her essential position within salvation. It had to be preserved clearly in the Church's witness before men, despite individual contrary teachings.

NOTES

1. *Expos. in Ps.* 5. – MG 55, 63.
2. Aberkios Inscription from the second century.
3. *Die Mariologie des hl. Thomas von Aquin* (Freiburg, 1.B. 1878), p. 67ff.
4. Eph. 5,26.
5. Ep. 49. – ML 16, 1203 D.
6. *In annunt. B.V.M. sermo* 2.
7. Eph. 5,27.
8. Denzinger (1794).
9. Ps. 44,14.
10. Mt. 9,12.
11. Pius XII, *Mystici corporis*, n. 23.
12. Rahner S.J., K., "Die Kirche der Suender," in: *Stimmen der Zeit*, 140 (1947), p. 172.
13. *Ibid.*, p. 168.
14. *Ibid.*, pp. 172f.
15. Sess. VI., can. 23 (Denz. 833).
16. *De natura et gratia.* – ML 44, 267.
17. *Exposito in salutationem angelicam.*
18. *De incarnatione*, lib. 14, cap.I, n.2.
19. *Loc. cit.*, n.13.

CHAPTER 8

Redemption of the Body

IT IS A CURIOUS FACT that in the first six centuries there is no explicitly established testimony on the mystery of Mary's Assumption into Heaven. Nonetheless, the mystery was celebrated in the earliest feast dedicated to her. The Church's inner life, as always, is aptly expressed by her liturgy. Her consciousness of faith had no sooner noted that —except for Christ—Mary is the only human being dwelling body and soul in eternal glory in Heaven, when she took the mystery into her heart and festively praised God with it down through the centuries. The definition of the dogma in 1950 gives evidence of no uncertainty about this point. It simply testifies to the fact that the mystery was accepted as self-evident and as undisputed in every age.

The inner foundation attributed to the mystery in the development of theology is less unique and clear. The many theologians who take the divine motherhood as the basic Mariological principle attribute Mary's Assumption to this mystery. This reasoning cannot offer the mystery of the Assumption anything more than a certain "aptness." Another school of thought cites the physical integrity of the perpetual Virgin as the inner foundation of her Assumption and preservation from disintegration. In this reasoning the connection is—at best—that some common third ele-

ment may serve as the foundation of both integral bodily
virginity and the Assumption, rather than one following
upon the other through some inner necessity. Also listed
as a foundation have been Mary's outstanding holiness and
her unity with Christ. Here too there is reason. Her holiness would appear to be the divine power that kept her soul
free from sin and gave her the highest graces. The assumption of her body, accordingly, seems a grace added by God
consonant with His power and love. Here, too, the foundation would be sought in a third point explaining why God
endowed Mary's soul, and body as well, with such extraordinary graces. The theologians' lack of unanimity on the
foundation of the Mystery of the Assumption is not a sign
of uncertainty regarding the fact itself. Quite the contrary.
The fact itself is firmly held despite the divergences in its
theological explanation. This proves well enough that the
elucidation of the mystery stems from another source—
God's Revelation.

Of course we too intend to set the mystery of the Assumption into the framework of Mariology. Here, again,
we intend to make our clarifications in the light of Mary,
the Type of the Church. In this clarification we will be able
to abolish the suspicion that the Assumption is merely an
afterthought to the essentials of Mariology. We will abolish the notion that it is tacked on by pious fantasy following Mary beyond the grave, trying to snatch more glory for
her, whether or not it fits the rational pattern of theology.
The Mystery of the Assumption fits into the entire pattern
of Mariology very meaningfully. This is because it is
definitely not the invention of the imagination. The Divine

Logic, rather, has brought the harmony of Mary's tasks in salvation to a meaningful conclusion.

Mary's Assumption makes her physical glory evident. This leads us directly to contemplate the Church's visibility and corporeality. If Mary, the Archetype of the Church, was taken in bodily form to Heaven, we will have to investigate why the Church's visibility is part of its essence. But there is no doubt that the Church is essentially visible: "They err in a matter of divine truth who hold that the Church is invisible, intangible, something 'pneumatological,' as some say."[1] Thus we must now investigate how the Church's visibility is part of her essence; also, why Christ willed that His Church must be a visible community, the Body of Christ in a tangible, living unity.

There is a general feeling—an almost folkloric idea—that the human body acts only as an instrument of the soul, not very differently from the way workmen use their tools. This idea, of course, is most inaccurate—to say the least. In a certain sense, to be sure, man's physical nature can be looked upon as a tool by whose help the soul performs her functions. But it must never be forgotten that man's body and soul are two *substantiae incompletae* fashioned for each other. This means that the body was fashioned for the soul to be used as the soul's instrument. It also means that the soul is fashioned to reside in the body. It means that only when the two are combined is there a complete human being. Corporeality, therefore, is an *essential* part of man.

Similarly, the visible structure of the Church is an essential part, but not really in the sense of an instrument, of her divine life-principle. To be sure, present-day apologists tend to stress the following reasoning: The Church must be visible because that is the only way her divine life can be imparted to men. Man is limited by his senses. He needs ears to hear God's Revelation; he needs eyes to see whence God's authority comes. This need has certainly come to fruition in the Church. To make it the decisive element, however, would be to take too pragmatic a view of the Church's visibility. The limitations of this reasoning are easily proved by many a man being able to feel himself religious and close to God without relying on any claims of the Church's audible and visible unity.

The real fact is that the Church is visible according to her very essence. Everything which is to participate in Redemption must be included in the Church. If Redemption is relegated only to the realm of the spirit, the idea is being interpreted in a sense much too spiritualistic, not unlike the idealistic tendency that looks upon the soul as the only reality (or at least the only important one). Matter and the bodily world become at most a burden to the soul and the soul must struggle for release and freedom. St. Paul said: "Who will deliver me from the body of this death?"[2] This passage has been falsely interpreted. Consequently, there has been a tendency to look upon asceticism as the conquest of the physical world. But St. Paul's words (and other similar passages of the New Testament) do not refer to the body or the material world as such, of which St. John said that "a new heaven and a new earth"[3] would be created. Rather, the allusion is to the somatic body, not yet enlivened by a soul in grace; a body, consequently, which has not received any part in Christ's Redemption through a soul in the state of grace.

The sub-spiritual cosmos, man's corporeal nature, and the material world are all destined to participate in Redemption, just as they participate in the curse of original sin. The cosmos was put under the curse in primordial times, although not through any fault of its own. Lacking freedom it could not sin. It came under the curse "by reason of him who made it subject";[4] that is, by man, who drew his own corporeal nature and the entire cosmos into his rebellion and resulting condemnation. Now creation, the physical world, waits for "the revelation of the children of God." It waits groaning for redeemed men to reveal themselves within the physical world and draw it into the Redemption.

This can only take place in the Church because all Redemption takes place in the Redeemer's Mystical Body which is the Church. Any person or thing that is to be redeemed can be so only through the Church. They must be drawn into the Church and constitute her essence. This is the reason why the Church must have her bodily component. The physical cosmos must be included. The Church must be visible, tangible, sensory, material—not only spiritual. Once corporeality has been included in the Church it ceases to be "the body of this death." The somatic body becomes "pneumatic," a body enlivened by the Spirit of Christ. The physical nature of the world becomes the *sacramentum*, the covering with the Divine Life of grace. The more grace reigns in the Church and in her individual members, the closer the body will participate in the Redemption. Christ does not dwell in His glory without His Body. So too the Church will not be without her physical component when she enters with her members into perfection. The Redemption will be completely achieved only when the Church with her members enters Heaven, that is, "when a new heaven and a new earth" have come into being.

The material world's completed redeemed state must also shine forth in Mary as Archetype of the Church. The essential point of view by which Mary is seen as the Type of the Church is as follows: Mary typifies the essence of the Church, a community of men and the Mystical Body of Christ, in whom the Divine Life of Christ dwells. This life is to be given to everyone who has been incorporated into this Body as a living member. The Church has performed her receptive co-redemption in Mary, her representative. It is in Mary that the Church has fully received her Redemption.

It follows, therefore, that the body must be seen in its perfected redeemed state in Mary. This does not mean that her body could have avoided passing through the dark portal of death. Every human being assumes completely the work of Redemption and its fruits of grace when, by dying, he gives his whole existence back to God the Father. Mary fulfilled this subjective, receptive and co-redeeming role of the Church when, by dying, she made Christ's redemptive death her own and subjectively co-enacted it. Historically speaking we know nothing about Mary's death. Yet it appears quite logical and the result of her position as Archetype of the receptive, co-redeeming Church. Christ made the final surrender and fulfillment of His human Will to the Will of His Father by His sacrificial death. In a perfect act of obedience, His recognition of God's sovereignty contrasted with Adam's disobedience. Every sacrifice is a surrender of man, of his entire being and existence, to God. When, because of man's insufficiency, these sacrifices are inadequate—like those which the Old Testament performed in anticipation of the true Sacrifice—the offerings made are symbols of a surrender of the whole human existence. In His true Sacrifice, Christ surrendered Himself in His full reality; it was a redemptive submission to God's sovereignty, offered for all men who had revolted against Him and who could no longer approach Him. To be effective, this sacrificial death has, of course, to be assumed by men. This can be done in no more perfect way than when man surrenders his own being completely to the Father. It will be taken from him anyway when he dies; man cannot prevent physical death. Morally, however, he can renounce the death with which he is burdened. Man can liken himself to the dying Redeemer, sacrificing and thus receiving Christ's redeeming death. Man's own death becomes thereby co-redemptive.

Mary died too, as Archetype of the co-redemptive Church. The Church day by day has to make Christ's death her own. It is she who constantly, continually dies with Christ and therefore rises with Him to eternal life. Mary is the perfect expression of the Church's co-redemptive work. Therefore it is most fitting that she should have died as did her Redeemer, both by her constant moral affirmation and by a physical, bodily death.

At the same time the redeemed state of the physical cosmos at the end of time shines forth in her body. In her body she co-enacted subjectively Christ's death. In her, as Archetype, her body shows the Church's fully redeemed body. Her body lights the way for the body of the Church and shows that the transfiguration dwells like a seed within her corporeality.

As Archetype of the Redeemed Church Mary must carry and reveal Redemption both "intensively" and "extensively" within her. Intensively, as Archetype, she has to be in the fullest possession of the grace given by Christ's Redemption that makes her what she is. We too are bearers on this earth of the divine life of grace. "We know that we have passed from death to life," St. John writes.[5] For us, however, this is still veiled. It is something which we do not experience but rather believe. St. Paul calls it a pledge,[6] essentially what we will later possess in Heaven, but which we still await in its unfolding and fulfillment. Mary, however, has to possess divine life completely unfolded because as Archetype she depicts the Church's essence as redeemed.

The incomplete state of Redemption that we as persons possess on earth accounts for the fact that our bodies have not as yet been drawn into complete Redemption. "Another law in my members wars against the law of my mind."[7] A man filled with grace can still cry out, "Who will deliver me from the body of this death!"[8] Great effort is needed to govern the body through the redeemed soul, and to reveal the soul's sonship of God through the body. Yet we have seen it is of the essence of the Church that the bodily sphere should also be redeemed and included in the Church. The redeemed state of the body will be perfected in eternity after the resurrection of the flesh.

Mary too must therefore extensively and typically reveal the essence of the Redeemed Church; that is, in its extension embracing the bodily element. She must completely

represent and signify in every respect the hidden fundamental reason of the Church as the redeemed Bride of
Christ. This is why the Church believes that her Archetype
dwells body and soul in perfection. Mary, the highest
representative and Archetype of the Church, brought her
body and soul to the Bridegroom to be redeemed. Now she
must stand in eternity next to the God-man-Bridegroom
revealing to the faithful that this soul and body belong to
the one whom Christ has "sanctified and healed in the water
by means of the Word and made into a Church in all her
glory, not having a spot or wrinkle or any such thing, but
rather that she might be holy and without blemish."[9] She
reveals to the faithful that they themselves are the living
stones[10] of this Church, of the great temple of the Holy
Spirit on earth. Their own bodies, too, are the temple
of the Holy Spirit, as St. Paul so profoundly remarked.[11]

Therefore we see that it is essential that Mary should
have entered into perfection, both in body and soul. Christ
dwells in eternal transfiguration in His whole humanity. He
earned this transfiguration for His entire Mystical Body.
But the Mystical Body received its personal oneness and
archetypical stature in Mary. She stands beside her Bridegroom as the Archetype of His Church. She receives the
fullness of life from Him and passes it on to the Church. St.
Thomas Aquinas, too, sees the reason for Mary's bodily
assumption in the fact that Mary is completely filled with
the grace of the Redemption. Thus, she stands beside Christ
whose whole Body shares in the splendor of the Resurrection. But this whole risen Body is Christ and the Church,
or, as St. Thomas says, Christ and Mary: "The particle of
the offering at Mass dropped into the Chalice points to the

risen Body, namely Christ and the most Blessed Virgin."[12]
In another place he says: "Some participate fully in blessed-
ness—that is, Christ Himself with His risen Body and the
Blessed Virgin."[13]

NOTES

1. Pius XII, *Mystici corporis*, n. 14.
2. Rom. 7, 24.
3. Apoc. 21, 1.
4. Rom. 8, 19–22.
5. 1 John 3, 14.
6. 2 Cor. 1, 22.
7. Rom. 7, 23.
8. Rom. 7, 24.
9. Eph. 5, 26f.
10. 1 Peter 2, 5.
11. 1 Cor. 1, 16.
12. *S. th.* III, q.83, a 5.
13. *In Sent.* IV. dist. 12, q. 1, a. 3, sol. 3.

Conclusion

In the pages of this book we have tried to present (by intellectual analysis and its theoretical consequences) an idea that has been affirmed for centuries in the life and devotion of the Church. We see Mariology very closely connected with the Church and thus we believe this exposition merely clarifies a fact that has flowed with the force of life itself through the centuries—the veneration of Mary. A number of conclusions can be drawn from our presentation and these contribute toward making a judgment on this amazingly potent phenomenon which dominates the history of the Church. Outside and even inside the Church, people may differ on the value attributed to the veneration of Mary. As a fact, however, it can never be passed over. Its potency, moreover, is due to the fact that it draws its strength like a vital power that flows from an innermost essence. Perhaps the idea of Mary as Archetype of the Church has clarified the reasons for this phenomenon more clearly than any other mystery of Mariology.

Veneration for Mary time and time again has been looked upon as a specific sign of the Catholic Christian. The reason behind this cannot be attributed to external happenstance. We hope that our exposition demonstrates that the crucial importance of Mary's veneration is founded in the essence of the Church and in the essence of Mary herself. Devotion to Mary is most natural to the Catholic Christian because of his understanding of the Church which manifests its particular stamp in her.

Since the time of the Council of Ephesus especially, Mary's universal veneration within the Church has been undisputed and incontestable. Historical testimonies are most explicit. In the testimony of the first two centuries, as we have shown, Mary was more an object of theological speculation than of liturgical or personal devotion. Yet the way this difference emerges lends itself precisely to demonstrating her position in the economy of salvation, thereby providing an explanation for the tremendous growth of her veneration in later times. Mary, as the one who imparts salvation to the world (in the sense we have outlined), stands, as God intended her, as the Archetype of the Church which imparts salvation. The Fathers received this knowledge from the treasures of Revelation. From thence it spread into the Church's awareness of her faith. Here it remains anchored and spreads into the vital life of ecclesiastical devotion, liturgical veneration and prayers of supplication.

Theology has a concept, *hyperdulia*, that contrasts Mary's veneration with that of other saints. This terminology is justified from the vantage point where we view Mary, for to her is due a specific, not merely a graduated, distinction from the *dulia* paid other saints. At first glance the *hyper* seems to refer merely to the overwhelming veneration Mary has received in history. No other saint, indeed, has had such devotion. Neither does any other saint stand as Mary does before man, encompassing so much, enriched by all virtues, accessible to all needs and drawing hearts from all parts of the world to herself.

Actually, the "more" (by which Mary's veneration surpasses that of all the saints) is based on meaningful facts and interrelations. Yet, theologians have never really unanimously answered the question whether the difference is one of degree or quality. The answer would seem to lie in our previous expositions. The act of veneration, like any other moral act, is determined by its object. The object through and under which veneration is given to Mary is specifically different from any other veneration of saints. Mary is revered as a saint in the usual sense, but in a special grade and measure. The devotion shown her is also an affirmation of what she really is: the Archetype of the Church in the full sense herein developed. This distinguishes her essentially from all other saints in whom the basic holiness of the Church is recognized and honored in a way different than in Mary's case.

The essential attitude and work of the Church shines forth in concrete reality in every saint. Man is holy to the extent that he realizes the essence of the Church in his own personal existence. Thus, holiness—the redeemed state of the Church—is the formal foundation for the veneration of saints. But in a sense the Church in her essential holiness is prior to the saints. The saint, a part and member of the Church, participates in her holiness and embodies it in his person. In other words, the saint has received his grace and holiness only because of and to the extent that he has been incorporated into the Church that existed before him.

Mary also personifies the holiness of the Church. She is

the germ-cell of the Church. She carries within her the Church's entire holiness to impart it to the Church assembled. She is the pre-existing Church; she is prior to all saints and to individual members of the Church. Mary is also the idea of the Church, the idea brought into existence in redeemed and co-redeeming humanity. Therefore, in an "ordinary" saint the Church reveres the effect of her essential holiness; it is glad of her own fecundity so distinctly evident in a given human being. In Mary, however, the Church affirms her own holy, co-redemptive and redeemed essence. She gratefully recognizes in Mary her own self in origin and beginning.

Thus, the veneration of Mary is the Church's testimony to herself. (This, of course, is also true of the other saints but in a lesser degree.) The veneration is a testimony to the Church's own essence and to her task of imparting salvation. This testimony should not be interpreted so much in an idealistic or theological sense as in an existential way. In Mary the Church sees herself as a person and she venerates her essence not in the abstract but in the fullblooded reality of the joy of her festal celebrations: "Let us all rejoice in the Lord that we celebrate this feast honoring the Blessed Virgin Mary." This is the theme of Mary's feast days.

From this point of view there can be no contradiction between Marian piety and dedication to Christ. In the subjective consciousness of the faithful, differences may arise as to their choice of this or that devotional preference within the over-all reality. Our age of analysis has dissolved the living complex of ecclesiastical devotion and forgotten that the most it can do is take apart, piece by piece, a reality that lives only in its complexity. The single-mindedness of the analysts of piety has not contributed to the enriching of religious life. Vitality began to be restored when the extremes began to come together again, that is, when the devout Christocentric man began to understand the meaning of Marian piety. Devotion to Christ is ultimately the acknowledgment of the person of Christ and His work that man makes his own. This attitude reached its perfection in Mary when she became the co-redemptive summit of the Church by her *fiat;* when she gave consent, as Archetype of the Church, to the Person and work of her Son. Therefore true devotion to Christ is Marian in attitude. When conscious veneration of Mary is added to devotion to Christ, the Marian attitude (identical with the essential attitude of the Church) is merely being further affirmed by prayer and liturgy.